T0341514

BASICS

# WATER CYCLES

\\ DORIS HAAS-ARNDT

BASICS

# WATER CYCLES

BIRKHÄUSER
BASEL · BOSTON · BERLIN

# CONTENTS

# FOREWORD

The availability of drinking water in buildings is taken for granted in developed, industrialized countries. Drinking water is, however, a valuable commodity, and is scarce in many parts of the world. The collection and treatment of drinking water are becoming increasingly expensive for industrialized countries and therefore also for the consumer. Similarly, the disposal and cleaning of waste water are becoming more resource-intensive and complex due to the substances it contains.

The interface between the drinking water and waste water is the distribution, use and disposal of water within buildings, a significant component of the architect's design. The arrangement of supply and disposal pipework and the technical requirements influence the location of sanitary and kitchen areas. Avoiding high water consumption is an important aspect of technical building services planning.

A broad knowledge of the requirements and possibilities for reducing water consumption is necessary to be able to take these key topics into account in the design of a building, right from its inception. This includes, above all, an understanding of the interrelationships and dependencies, as well as technical systems. It is important to think of the water cycle in a building as an integral part of the design.

The volume *Basics Water Cycles* is aimed at students of architecture and recent graduates without previous knowledge of building services. With the aid of easy-to-understand introductions and explanations, the reader is taken through the subject matter step by step. The path of water through the various zones of a building is described and related to their specific roles and requirements, so that students are able to fully understand the interrelationships and introduce them into their own designs.

Bert Bielefeld, Editor

# INTRODUCTION

Part of the technical services in a modern building is a complex pipe-work system for supplying drinking water and disposing of waste water. This system is a cycle, somewhat similar to the natural water cycle: fresh water is collected, supplied to the building, distributed through a pipe-work system, and heated if required. It is piped to the draw-off points in bathrooms, kitchens and other sanitary rooms. As soon as it leaves the drinking water pipe through the faucet, it becomes waste water and flows through the waste water pipework into the sewers, from where it is cleaned again and finally returned to natural watercourses. Architects must integrate this cycle into the design of their buildings, as without a carefully planned and properly functioning fresh and waste water system, WCs cannot be flushed, washing machines cannot be operated, and no water will emerge from a shower.

The chapters that follow consider the individual positions of water in a building along the water cycle, and describe the functions of the elements connected to this cycle. It should become clear how a drinking water supply system works, how it is designed into a building, and which aspects should be taken into account. There is also an explanation of how waste water is created and conducted into the drainage system, the general problems that arise in the supply and disposal of water, and the options for their solution.

# WATER SUPPLY

Approximately two thirds of the earth's surface is covered with water. Of this, only 0.3% is fresh water and therefore potential drinking water. Drinking water is very high-quality fresh water that is suitable for human consumption.

### THE NATURAL WATER CYCLE

The natural water cycle—or hydrologic cycle—is a continuous sequence of evaporation, precipitation, and rainwater draining into bodies of open water or seeping into the ground to accumulate as groundwater. Water vapor rises under the influence of solar radiation or other heating effects to form clouds, and falls as precipitation back onto the earth's surface. Some of the rainwater that seeps away is absorbed by the ground, some evaporates, and some is taken up into plants by capillary action. A proportion reaches the lower soil strata and helps maintain the groundwater table. › Fig. 1

Groundwater

Groundwater is described as precipitation water that is stored on top of an impervious stratum and has a temperature of between 8 and 10 °C all year round. Groundwater is generally microbe-free and is pumped up to the surface from deep wells. It provides about three quarters of our drinking water, and goes through several stages of cleaning and filtering before it is fed into the public supply network.

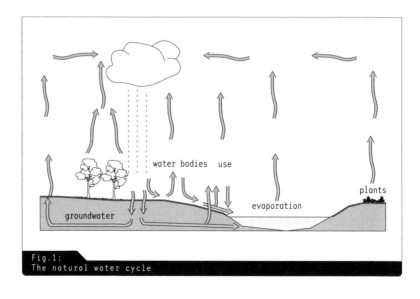

Fig.1:
The natural water cycle

Substantial groundwater extraction and extensive sealing of urban land surfaces have a substantial impact on the natural water cycle. Rainwater falling on impervious areas cannot seep naturally into groundwater, but is conducted directly into bodies of open water or into the drains. The groundwater table is greatly reduced by building developments, deforestation and drainage works.

In addition, the extensive extraction of groundwater for agriculture and industry, and the pollutants that these activities introduce, are harmful to the system. Pollutants from sources such as manure, agricultural pesticides, landfill, highway drainage and industrial emissions, which fall as acid rain and seep into the groundwater, are a serious cause for concern and can be removed only by expensive cleaning and filtering. The increasing contamination of water combined with high water usage produces an ecological imbalance, the consequences of which result in high costs.

### STANDARDS FOR DRINKING WATER

Drinking water intended for human consumption has to meet certain standards. It must be good to taste, odorless and colorless, and free of pathogens and microbes. Every draw-off point must provide best-quality drinking water at sufficient pressure. Quantities of chemicals added to disinfect the water, and of other possible constituents, must be kept within limits specified for European Union countries by an EU directive and regional drinking water regulations. The water's quality and the limits for the substances it contains are checked regularly in accordance with the applicable national standards for drinking water. These standards for drinking water quality change constantly. Today's level of pollution means they can be met only with great difficulty and at increasing cost.

Hardness level  Water with high calcium and magnesium content is described as hard, while water with low calcium and magnesium content is soft. High levels of hardness produce a build-up of mineral deposits in pipe networks; these deposits are known as scale. Considerably more detergent is required for washing clothes in hard water, and the dishwasher may leave

\\ Note:
Surfacings such as asphalt are impervious to water and effectively seal the ground, thus preventing groundwater from being replenished.

\\ Note:
The European Union Council Directive 98/83 (EU Drinking Water Directive) concerns the quality of drinking water for human consumption and obliges all member states to implement it stepwise into their national legislation.

| Hardness range | Hardness in mmol/l | Description |
| --- | --- | --- |
| 1 | < 1.3 | soft |
| 2 | 1.3–2.5 | medium hard |
| 3 | 2.5–3.8 | hard |
| 4 | > 3.8 | very hard |

a thin film of lime on the dishes. Water hardness is measured in mmol/l (millimoles per liter). The hardness level depends on the source of the water. › Tab. 1 Water with less than 30 mg/l calcium bicarbonate, on the other hand, does not allow the pipes to form a protective surface layer, with the result that the pipe material is attacked by acids, and corrodes. The effect of water hardness on health is insignificant.

pH

An important measure of the "aggressivity" of water is its pH (Latin: *potentia Hydrogenii*). The pH describes the concentration of hydrogen ions in water, or more precisely: the negative logarithm of the hydrogen ion concentration. On this scale, pure water has a pH of 7, i.e. there are $10^{-7}$ g H ions in one liter of pure water. If the pH drops below 7, the water behaves aggressively like an acid; if the pH is higher, the water behaves as a base (alkali) and more lime is deposited.

## THE DEMAND FOR DRINKING WATER

In the 19th century, Germany required about 30 l of drinking water per day per head for consumption and personal hygiene. Today, by contrast, the figure will soon reach 130 l, due to the increasing levels of sanitary convenience, such as flowing water, showers and flushing toilets. This consumption is doubtless very high, but it has already decreased, because a great number of water-saving fittings have been installed in bathrooms and WCs in recent years. However, industry, commerce and agriculture are using increasing amounts of water. The irrigation of agricultural land consumes the largest quantity of drinking water worldwide.

In the industrialized countries, almost all buildings are connected to the public drinking water supply network. Many billion cubic meters of water are removed from the natural water cycle for drinking water supplies every year. Most of this comes from groundwater and bodies of open water, and the rest from sources such as river bank filtration. The term "bodies of open water" refers to rivers or lakes, the water of which is usually contaminated with bacteria and mechanically eroded solids, and can be supplied as drinking water only after a long purification process.

Conurbations and regions where water is scarce have to rely on some of their drinking water being transported from far away. At the same time, the high proportion of impervious surfaces in cities means most of the rainwater flows directly into their drainage systems. As it is particularly difficult to supply the quantities of drinking water required in these areas, it is imperative to reduce drinking water demand.

The daily drinking water demand of domestic households can be divided into different uses. The amount actually consumed is quite a small proportion of the total. Only about 5 l water are drunk or used for cooking, and the rest used for other purposes. Peaks and troughs during the day are compensated for by water storage at waterworks.

The average hot water demand in domestic residential properties is between 30 and 60 l per person per day. It can vary greatly from day to day and with the habits of the users. A bath requires about 120 to 180 l hot water at 40 °C; a 5-minute shower about 40 l at 37 °C. Energy and drinking water can be saved by choosing to have a shower instead of a bath.

### SAVING DRINKING WATER

Today there are many sanitary engineering solutions for saving drinking water: flow limiters in shower heads, water-saving faucets and toilets, and domestic appliances (e.g. washing machines and dishwashers)

Tab.2:
Typical usage of drinking water

| Activity | Usage in l/day/person |
|---|---|
| Drinking and cooking | 5 |
| Basic personal hygiene | 10 |
| Baths and showers | 38 |
| Dishwashing | 8 |
| Cleaning | 8 |
| Clothes washing | 15 |
| Toilet flushing | 40 |
| Garden watering | 6 |
| **Total** | **130** |

with reduced water consumption. Installing a water meter in each apartment instead of having one central metering point in the basement has a proven water-saving effect, because users can track their consumption directly; they just pay for the water they have used. WC cisterns with stop buttons and a water usage of 4–6 l per flush are now standard. More advanced systems such as vacuum toilets use 1.2 l water per flush. Composting toilets of various types use no water at all. › Chapter Drinking water systems in buildings, Sanitary rooms

A more accurate analysis of drinking water usage makes it clear that water of drinking water quality is required for only the smallest proportion of the total amount supplied. › Tab. 2 Pure drinking water is necessary only for personal hygiene, washing kitchenware, cooking and drinking. Rainwater-quality water is adequate for toilet flushing, cleaning, or watering the garden. Water consumption can therefore be substantially reduced by using rainwater. Cleaned gray water from showers and hand basins, for example, can also be used for flushing WCs. › Chapter Waste water, Uses of waste water

Merely installing modern water-saving faucets in sanitary rooms can reduce average drinking water demand to about 100 l per person per day. With a few more of the measures mentioned above, it would even be possible to manage on half of normal drinking water consumption with no significant loss of comfort.

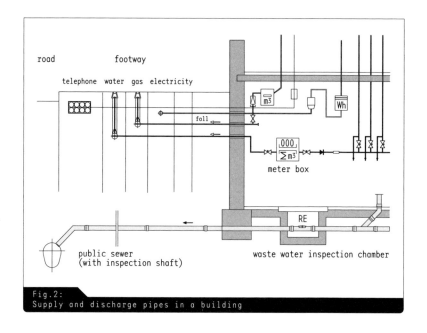

road    footway

telephone  water  gas  electricity

fall

m³

Wh

,000,
∑m³

meter box

RE

public sewer
(with inspection shaft)

waste water inspection chamber

Fig.2:
Supply and discharge pipes in a building

## DRINKING WATER SYSTEMS IN BUILDINGS

The water cycle normally begins in buildings with the supply of cold drinking water through a pipe connected to the public water supply network, unless the plot has its own private supply (well). In larger towns and settlements, the connection to the public drinking water supply is normally at a frost-free depth of between 1.00 and 1.80 m below the sidewalk. Each plot has its own drinking water service pipe, which heads off into the building at right angles to the public supply pipe, as far as the house connection or main stopcock and water metering point. › Fig. 2 In residential properties this pipe has a nominal diameter of about 25 mm (DN 25).

In some European countries, the position of the drinking water connection is marked with a colored sign on a nearby house wall for ease of identification and location of the connection point. The lines and numbers on the sign give the distance to the drinking water connection—from the sign—and the direction (to the right, left, in front or behind). The other abbreviations normally describe the type of connection; the accompanying numbers give the nominal internal pipe diameter.

To prevent microbes from flourishing, the drinking water supplied to the building is cold, i.e. between 5 and 15 °C. To obtain hot water, the

› 🗋

Water
temperature

drinking water must first be heated in the building. Hot water in this context is described as drinking water with a temperature of between 40 and 90 °C. For personal hygiene, a water temperature of 40 to 45 °C is adequate, while washing dishes requires water at 55 to 85 °C to produce hygienic results.

Water pressure The water supply company creates a pressure within the water supply network to distribute the drinking water. The water pressure of the public supply is usually between 6 and 10 bar, and is brought down to about 5 bar or less by pressure reducers in the building's pipework system.

> Chapter Drinking water systems in buildings, Components of a drinking water supply system

These values may vary from place to place and should only be taken as a guide. The absolute minimum pressure at the draw-off point should not fall below 0.5 bar, as otherwise the water cannot be distributed properly. Pressure losses in the pipework system may be caused by, for example, a great difference in height between the service pipe and the draw-off point. Loss of pressure can be taken roughly as 1 bar for every 10 m height.

## COMPONENTS OF A DRINKING WATER SUPPLY SYSTEM

Drinking water is distributed within a building's supply system through a branched network of horizontal and vertical pipes, which are normally concealed in service ducts, wall lining cavities, floor voids, or wall chases. Other water supply system components include a water meter to record consumption, safety devices, stop valves and draw-off points.

House connection The service pipe to the public water supply and the water meter are part of the supplied service and usually belong to the water supply company. The service pipe takes the shortest route into the building and must not be built over, so that it can easily be located and repaired if necessary. For safety reasons, the pipe duct must pass through the outside wall or foundation of the building at right angles, and the pipe must be enclosed by a protective sleeve.

◧

\\ Note:
The abbreviation DN, which is used as a label in every pipework drawing, means "diamètre nominal" and defines the nominal internal diameter of a pipe. This must comply with national regulations and depends on the size of the system.

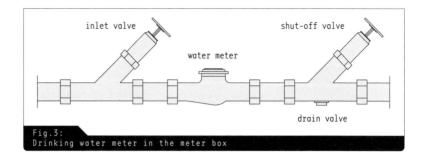

inlet valve

shut-off valve

water meter

drain valve

Fig.3:
Drinking water meter in the meter box

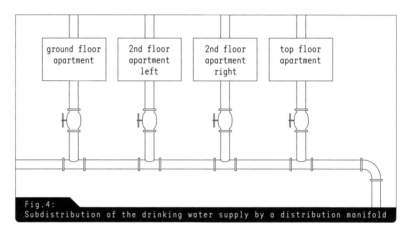

| ground floor apartment | 2nd floor apartment left | 2nd floor apartment right | top floor apartment |

Fig.4:
Subdistribution of the drinking water supply by a distribution manifold

Water meter

The calibrated water meter is positioned directly between the public water supply stopcock and the stopcock for the building's internal water pipework system. These two shut-off valves allow the meter to be removed without complications. › Fig. 3

The architect's design role starts at the water meter. The meter should be housed in a frost-free and readily accessible enclosure, e.g. in a meter box on the road side of the building, so that it can be read easily. If the meter cannot be installed inside the building, it may be housed in a meter chamber outside the building. This may even be specified so as to allow the meter to be read by the water supply company without the building occupant's being present.

Distribution manifold

If the drinking water distribution system has several risers (which may be required, for example, for supplying water to the different floors of an apartment block), a manifold is also incorporated to feed the individual apartments. › Fig. 4 In addition to the subdivision of the drinking water feed, there are often also heating supply pipes, separate draw-off points (e.g. outdoors) and, if necessary, separate pipes supplying water

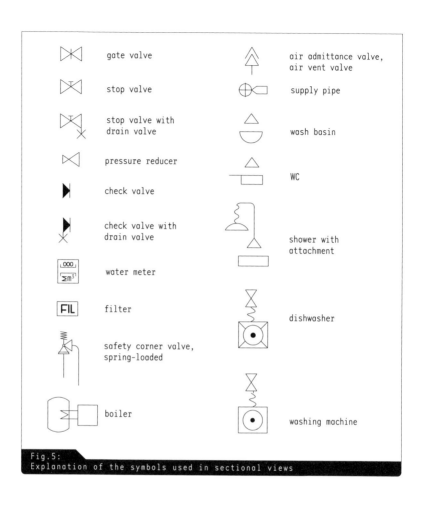

| | | | |
|---|---|---|---|
| ⋈ | gate valve | air admittance valve, air vent valve |
| ⋈ | stop valve | supply pipe |
| ⋈ | stop valve with drain valve | wash basin |
| ⋈ | pressure reducer | WC |
| ▶ | check valve | shower with attachment |
| ▶ | check valve with drain valve | dishwasher |
| water meter | | washing machine |
| FIL | filter | |
| | safety corner valve, spring-loaded | |
| | boiler | |

**Fig. 5:**
Explanation of the symbols used in sectional views

for firefighting. Each riser from the manifold is carefully labeled so that it is clear which pipe feeds which premises. Each riser network has its own shut-off valve so that replacement of system components can be carried out independently of the rest of the system.

### Layout drawings and symbols

European Standard EN 806 and its national annexes give special graphic symbols for system components and sanitary fixtures for use on design drawings of drinking water systems. They indicate the components to be installed in buildings and their spatial positioning and arrangement. › Fig. 5 These standards may vary from country to country. The system must be drawn in plan and sectional views to fully depict the drinking water system and its associated pipework. Since sanitary appliances in plan are

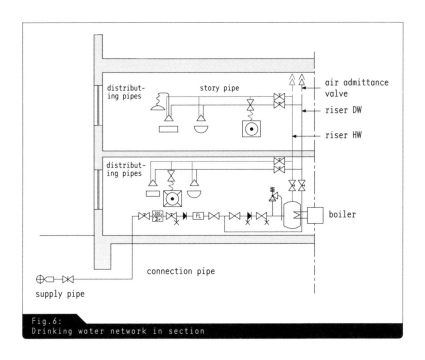

distribut-
ing pipes          story pipe              air admittance
valve

riser DW

riser HW

distribut-
ing pipes

boiler

connection pipe

supply pipe

Fig.6:
Drinking water network in section

seen from above, some appliances may require different symbols for plan and sectional views. A key on the drawing is generally helpful to explain the symbols used.

Representation
in section The representation of the system in section should be schematic and contain as much information about the drinking water system as possible. The sequence of the drinking water system symbols used should correspond to the actual arrangement of the sanitary items. Symbols and pipework are drawn as if the supply network and draw-off points were in the same, single plane. › Fig. 6

Representation
in plan When drawing the system in plan it is important to identify the rising and falling pipes separately with arrows showing the direction of flow in the pipes. › Fig. 7 You should also show whether a pipe begins, ends or carries through each story. › Fig. 8

**Description of pipework components**

Many pipework components in drinking water systems are referred to by special terms that are not used in other supply systems. › Fig. 6 The most important terms are:

_ service pipe for the pipe between the public supply and main stopcock in the building

20

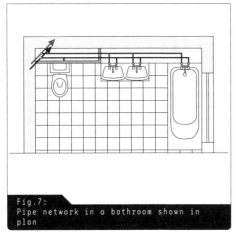

Fig.7:
Pipe network in a bathroom shown in plan

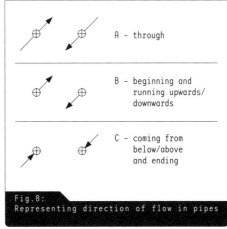

A - through

B - beginning and running upwards/downwards

C - coming from below/above and ending

Fig.8:
Representing direction of flow in pipes

_ <u>riser</u> for the pipe which passes vertically through the building, from which the

_ <u>pipes supplying the individual stories</u> branch off horizontally

_ <u>circulation pipe</u>, which provides continuous hot water at the draw-off points, but is not always required

_ <u>distributing pipes</u> are the vertical pipes branching from the horizontal pipes supplying each story to the draw-off points.

The internal diameter of risers in residential buildings is about DN 20, and for pipes supply stories about DN 15, i.e. nominal diameters of 20 and 15 mm respectively.

Circulation pipes

A circulation pipe ensures that hot water is available immediately at draw-off points. This has the advantage that a large amount of cold water does not have to flow through the pipe before the hot water appears, which is frequently the problem with instantaneous water heaters. A disadvantage is the electrical energy continuously consumed by the pump to keep the water circulating in the pipework. A time-switched pump, which only runs when hot water is needed, can mitigate the effect.

**Pipe routes**

Horizontal pipe routes may pass under a basement ceiling or be placed in the floor construction. Larger buildings often have floor ducts, or position the pipes above suspended ceilings. › Fig. 9 Vertical pipes in basements or equipment rooms may be fixed openly on the walls, › Fig. 10 and in the stories above in installation shafts or, for short lengths, be concealed in half-height false walls. › Chapter Drinking water systems in buildings, Sanitary rooms

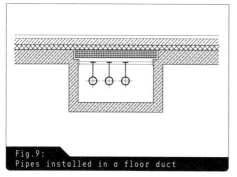

Fig.9:
Pipes installed in a floor duct

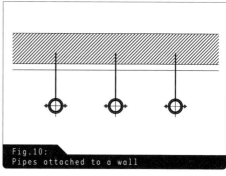

Fig.10:
Pipes attached to a wall

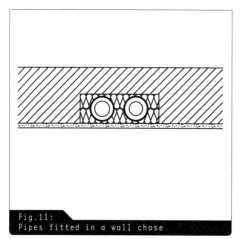

Fig.11:
Pipes fitted in a wall chase

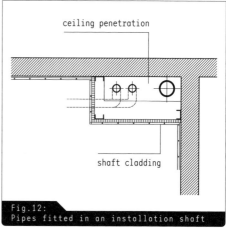

ceiling penetration

shaft cladding

Fig.12:
Pipes fitted in an installation shaft

In solid wall and floor construction, pipes are fitted into insulated wall chases, if the wall has a large enough cross section and there are no structural engineering reasons to preclude it. › Fig. 11 This method of installation is increasingly being superseded by installation shafts in sanitary rooms because of its complexity and poor sound insulation. › Fig. 12 False walls, in comparison with shafts, just clad the pipes in the wall cavity and generally terminate at half room-height, while an installation shaft can carry pipes through several stories. › Fig. 13

### Calculation of pipe sizes

The nominal diameter of the pipes is determined by the number of consumer points connected. › Tab. 3 It is also important to consider the probability of simultaneous draw-off, the material used for the pipes, the

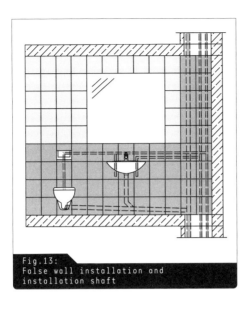

Fig.13:
False wall installation and
installation shaft

Tab.3:
Diameter of drinking water pipes

| Pipe type | Approximate internal diameter |
|-----------|-------------------------------|
| Service pipe | DN 25 to DN 32 |
| Riser | DN 20 |
| 1-5 draw-off points | DN 20 |
| 5-10 draw-off points | DN 25 |
| 10-20 draw-off points | DN 32 |
| 20-40 draw-off points | DN 40 |
| Story distribution pipes | DN 15 |
| 1 WC cistern | DN 10 to DN 15 |
| 1-2 wash basins | DN 15 |
| 1 shower | DN 15 |
| 1 bath | DN 20 to 25 |
| 1 garden hose | DN 20 to 25 |

pressure loss due to friction, and minimum flow pressure. The system must be designed to have a minimum flow pressure in the pipe such that the remotest drinking water draw-off point always has sufficient pressure to operate properly. The pipe friction pressure loss factor is the fall in pressure within a section of pipe divided by its length.

## Materials

Modern drinking water pipes that are in the ground outside the building are normally of plastic (polyethylene HD), because metal pipes require additional corrosion protection. A new development is the multi-layer metal composite pipe, which combines the advantages of metal (strength) and plastic (corrosion resistance).

Copper, galvanized steel, stainless steel or plastic (polyethylene) are used inside the building as materials for drinking water pipes. Plastic pipes are not rigid and their small cross section and ability to be bent to tight radii allows them to be installed even within a floor construction. Polyethylene pipes are usually designed as a pipe-in-pipe system: the flexible drinking water pipe (PE-X) is surrounded by an additional flexible, external protective pipe (PE-HD), and can be taken out of the protective pipe and replaced if necessary. As well as their high flexibility, plastic pipes have the advantage of resistance to scale and corrosion. When metal pipes are used or when pipework is replaced as part of a refurbishment project, attention should be paid to placing the less noble material after the more noble material (relative to the direction of flow), e.g. copper after steel, as otherwise corrosion could occur.

## Safety devices

Most systems incorporate safety measures to maintain the high quality of their drinking water. The quality must not be reduced by the entry of non-potable water, for instance. These devices include safety fittings that prevent back-flow or suction of contaminated water and the mixing of drinking water with water of lesser quality, which may happen, for example, if there is underpressure in the system due to a pipe developing a leak at the same time as a shower head has been left in bathwater. These safety devices prevent the underpressure from sucking bathwater into the drinking water supply.

\\ Note:
Polyethylene HD is also used for buried pipes; PE-X is used mainly for internal pipework with a protective outer covering of PE-HD. HD means high density, PE-X crosslinked polyethylene.

\\ Note:
The maintenance of purity of drinking water in buildings is governed by European Standard EN 1717, "Protection against pollution of potable water in water installations and general requirements of devices to prevent pollution by backflow".

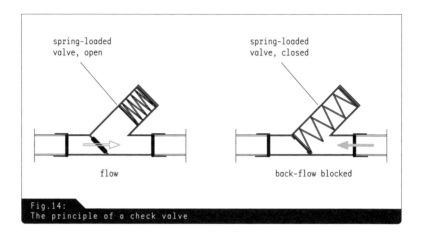

spring-loaded
valve, open

spring-loaded
valve, closed

flow

back-flow blocked

Fig.14:
The principle of a check valve

Check valves

One of the safety devices normally built into a domestic water installation is a check valve placed after the water meter. It is a self-closing, spring-loaded valve that prevents the backflow of drinking water in the pipe. The check valve opens only to allow water through in the correct direction of flow. If the flow stops, it closes again. If the direction of flow reverses, the valves closes with increased pressure. › Fig. 14

Air admittance valve

Check valves are normally installed in combination with an air admittance valve, which acts to compensate any underpressure occurring in the pipework system and prevent back-suction of contaminated water into the drinking water supply. The air admittance valve is positioned at the highest point in every cold or hot water riser. The valve inside the air admittance valve is normally closed. › Fig. 15 In conjunction with the check valve, the air admittance valve opens when underpressure occurs, and the inward flow of air prevents used water from being sucked back into the pipework. › Fig. 16

As there is a risk of water escaping from the air admittance valve when there is overpressure in the pipework, the valve may be connected to a drip collection pipe, which drains any escaping water into the waste water pipework and thus into the sewer. A drip collection pipe is not required if the air admittance valve is positioned above a shower or basin, where any escaping water cannot cause any damage.

Pressure reducer

The water pressure provided by the water supply company may be too high for normal draw-off points and may need to be reduced by a pressure reducer inside the building. The delivery pressure acts on a moving diaphragm, which either opens or closes a connected spring valve, depending on the setting. › Fig. 17 The pressure reducer should be installed in a position where it can be easily maintained.

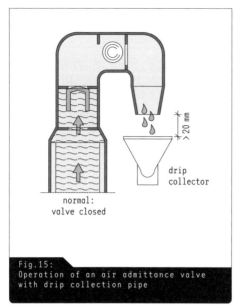

> 20 mm

drip
collector

normal:
valve closed

Fig.15:
Operation of an air admittance valve
with drip collection pipe

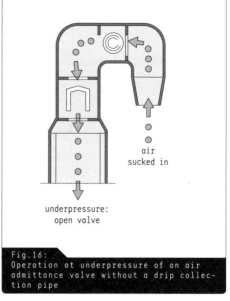

air
sucked in

underpressure:
open valve

Fig.16:
Operation at underpressure of an air
admittance valve without a drip collection pipe

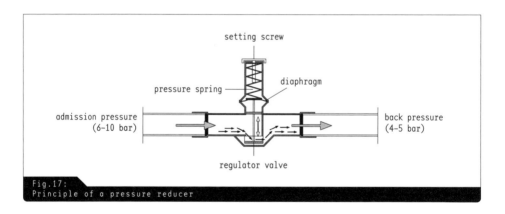

setting screw

pressure spring

diaphragm

admission pressure
(6–10 bar)

back pressure
(4–5 bar)

regulator valve

Fig.17:
Principle of a pressure reducer

Filter

     A fine filter is built into every drinking water system to ensure that it is free of dirt and rust particles. In most cases it is installed between the water meter and the pressure reducer, so that the latter is not contaminated. Installing a filter is worthwhile only if it is regularly serviced, because a filter insert cannot be expected to remain permanently free of microbes.

Safety
distances

     Buried drinking water pipes should be placed more than 1 m from any wastewater pipes above them, so as to prevent contamination of the

26

| Pipe | Insulation thickness |
|---|---|
| _ In the open in an unheated space | 4 mm |
| _ In an installation shaft with no nearby pipes carrying hot water | |
| _ In a wall chase | |
| _ In the open in a heated space | 9 mm |
| _ In an installation shaft with nearby pipes carrying hot water | 13 mm |

The insulation thickness is calculated assuming a thermal conductivity of 0.035 W/m$^2$K and must be recalculated for other insulation materials

drinking water supply in the event of a leak. If it is not possible to maintain this safety distance, the drinking water pipe must be laid above the waste water pipe, at a distance of at least 20 cm.

Thermal
insulation

Cold drinking water pipes should be prevented from inadvertent heating from nearby hot water or heating pipes by insulating them, or by maintaining a suitable distance to keep them free of microbes. Drinking water pipes should also be insulated when they pass through heated spaces. › Tab. 4

HOT WATER SYSTEMS

To satisfy the daily demand for hot water, part of the drinking water in a building is heated before being distributed. Hot water supply systems consist of the cold water feed, a boiler, perhaps a hot water storage tank, hot water distribution pipes leading to draw-off points, and in some circumstances circulation pipes, which ensure that hot water is instantly available at the draw-off points.

\\ Important:
Cold water pipes should always be fixed below gas pipes, as there is always a risk that condensing water could cause corrosion of the gas pipe and result in a dangerous gas leak.

Tab.5:
Conventional insulation thicknesses for hot water pipes

| Nominal pipe diameter | Insulation thickness |
|---|---|
| _ up to DN 20 | 20 mm |
| _ from DN 22 to DN 35 | 30 mm |
| _ from DN 40 to DN 100 | pipe DN |
| _ larger than DN 100 | 100 mm |

Half the above thickness is adequate for pipe lengths of up to 8 m
_ at wall and ceiling penetrations
_ where pipes cross

Pipe layout

If a building obtains its hot water from a central installation, the hot water pipes mainly run parallel to the cold water pipes throughout the building and have more or less the same pipe cross section. The water temperature in the pipework is between 40 and 60 °C. To avoid energy losses, the hot water pipes should be kept as short as possible and always thermally insulated where they pass through unheated spaces. The extra space required for insulation must be taken into account when designing the pipework route.

The insulation thickness is approximately equal to the pipe diameter; with pipes less than 8 m long, half that thickness is adequate. This is also the case where pipes pass through walls or ceilings and where they cross, e.g. in the floor construction. › Tab. 5

Individual, group or central hot water supply

Hot water systems can be central or decentralized in the building or provide hot water directly at the draw-off point. If a hot water source has only one draw-off point connected to it, this arrangement is called an individual supply, while with several connected draw-off points it is a group supply. › Figs. 18 and 19 With a central supply all draw-off points are supplied with hot water from a single, central boiler. › Fig. 20 It is also possible to combine individual, group and central systems, for example to switch off a central boiler in summer and yet have hot water available through individual supply points.

Boilers

There are basically two types of boilers used to provide hot water: continuous flow or instantaneous water heaters, which heat the water directly as it is used; and storage water heaters, which keep the water constantly hot and ready for drawing off. A further difference between the types relates to the source of heat. Heat sources include solid fuel, oil, gas, electricity, geothermal, and solar energy. Heating takes place either indirectly through a heat exchanger and a heat medium, or directly by the application of heat to the water to be heated.

› 🛢

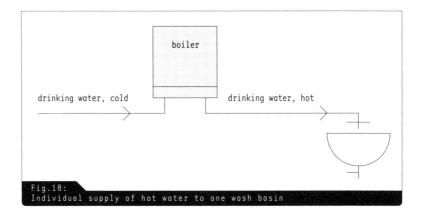

Fig.18:
Individual supply of hot water to one wash basin

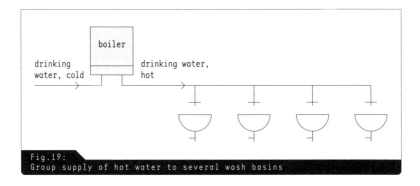

Fig.19:
Group supply of hot water to several wash basins

If possible, boilers installed in a central plant are used to heat the building and supply it with hot water. The plant consists of a hot water storage vessel, which stores service water and provides a source of heat for the heating circuit, and a connected boiler, which releases its heat to the service water. Hot water and heating energy are transported

\\ Note:
A heat exchanger is used to transfer heat from one medium into another. The heat medium could be water, which releases its heat into the air, for example, as with a radiator. In hot water supply systems the heat exchanger is inside the hot water storage vessel.

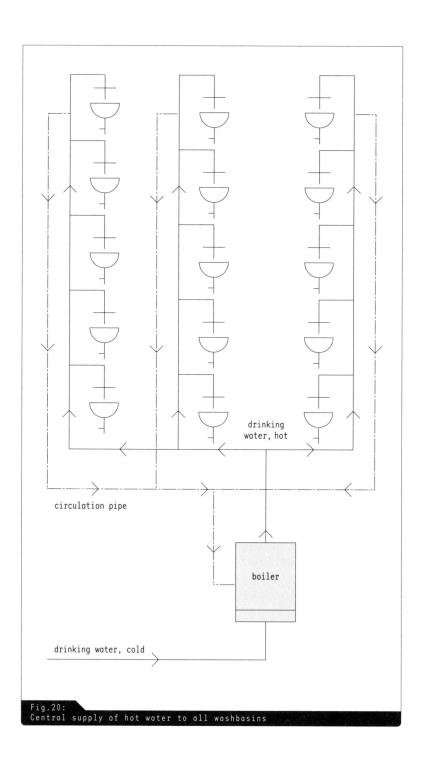

drinking water, hot

circulation pipe

boiler

drinking water, cold

Fig.20:
Central supply of hot water to all washbasins

by pumps through the pipe network to the draw-off points and heating radiators. Central plants have the advantage that a solar thermal energy installation can be connected or retrofitted at a later date and contribute to supplying hot water to the hot water storage vessel.

### Continuous flow systems

Continuous flow systems, also called instantaneous or continuous flow water heaters, heat the water directly to a temperature of about 60 °C. › Fig. 21 Their advantage is that only the amount of hot water needed is heated. In contrast to storage systems, there are no standby heat losses with continuous flow systems, and the water cannot generally be classed as fresh.

Continuous flow water heaters are inexpensive to install and save space. They are highly efficient because they heat the water directly. The startup phase cannot be avoided: hot water can be supplied to the draw-off point only after a delay, which results in fresh water flowing unused with the waste water into the sewers. The pipes from the instantaneous water heater to the draw-off points should be as short as possible, so that this cold water phase is curtailed. It cannot be completely eliminated, however.

Instantaneous water heaters can be operated with electricity or gas. Electrical systems generally use an AC supply, while the gas systems require a flue or chimney connection. Electrically powered instantaneous water heaters are associated with high energy costs. As electricity is very expensive to produce, its use as an energy carrier should be restricted to providing small quantities of water or to situations when no other energy carrier can reasonably be considered. Gas, on the other hand, although it is a fossil fuel, produces the least amount of carbon dioxide ($CO_2$) of all the fossil energy carriers.

› ◧

If designed as gas combination boilers, instantaneous water heaters can supply hot water and heating energy at the same time in a suitable system. Water quantities can be controlled hydraulically, thermally or electronically. Continuous flow systems can serve several draw-off points

◧

\\ Note:
Coal, oil and gas are fossil fuels. When burned they produce carbon dioxide ($CO_2$) and contribute to global warming. There will also come a time when they are finally used up and are no longer available as energy sources.

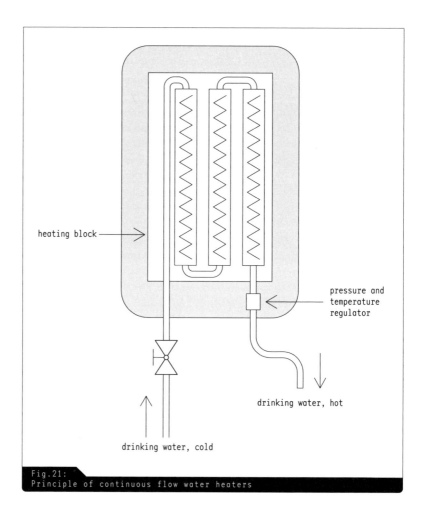

heating block

pressure and
temperature
regulator

drinking water, hot

drinking water, cold

Fig.21:
Principle of continuous flow water heaters

simultaneously and are used for individual, group and central hot water
supplies. Maximum water flow is limited, however; when there is a high
simultaneous draw-off, such as might be the case for hotels or sports halls,
the output of a continuous system is too low. In this case a central storage
system should be used.

Instantaneous
water heater
with integrated
water storage

Another hybrid form is an instantaneous water heater with a small,
integral hot water reservoir holding between 15 to 100 l water. If more
water is needed, e.g. for a bath, the rest of the bathwater is heated as if by
an instantaneous water heater. Continuous flow systems with integrated

# Your opinion is important to us

1. Please list the author and title of the book you purchased:

2. Please rate the book in the following areas:
1 = very good, 5 = poor

|  | 1 | 2 | 3 | 4 | 5 |
|---|---|---|---|---|---|
| Up-to-date | | | | | |
| Accurate | | | | | |
| Practical | | | | | |
| Language is clear and comprehensible | | | | | |
| Visual presentation (layout) | | | | | |
| Quality of illustrations/tables | | | | | |
| Organization, didactic approach | | | | | |
| Value for money | | | | | |

3. How could the book be improved?

4. In which of the following areas do you have the greatest need for information?

- Design
- Technical Drawing
- Construction
- Profession
- Building Physics/Building Services
- Design Aesthetics
- Materials
- Landscape Architecture
- Town Planning
- Theory

5. What is a subject in which you feel a good textbook or reference work is still lacking?

6. Do you have any other comments? ...please send them to: feedback@birkhauser.ch

7. How did you find out about this book?
- Colleague
- Teacher
- Bookstore
- Publisher's catalogue
- Publisher's prospectus
- Journal
- Internet
- Review in
- Ad in
- Other

Nicht frankieren
Ne pas affranchir

Non affrancare
No stamp required

**A**

RÉPONSE PAYÉE
SUISSE

**Birkhäuser**
Viaduktstrasse 42
4051 Basel
Schweiz

**A** *PRIORITY*
PRIORITAIRE

**Sender:**

**E-Mail:**

**I am**

A student

A teacher

I would like to be kept informed of the publisher's future publications.

Are you interested in becoming a Birkhäuser author?
If so, please contact the editorial department.

All of the cards we receive are entered in a semiannual prize drawing for five Birkhäuser books.
Results of the drawing are final and legal recourse is excluded.
Winners will be notified by us.

www.birkhauser.ch

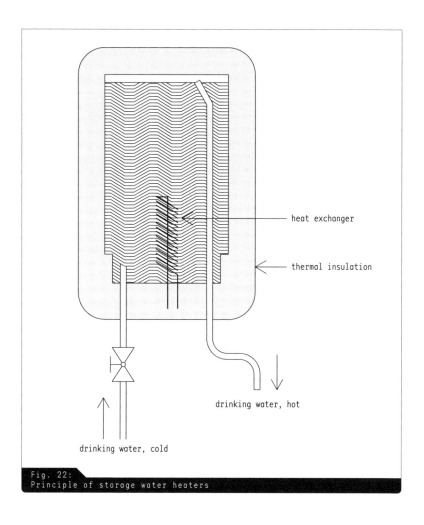

heat exchanger

thermal insulation

drinking water, hot

drinking water, cold

Fig. 22:
Principle of storage water heaters

storage are mainly used to supply smaller housing units with hot water and heating energy.

### Storage systems

These storage water heaters continuously heat the hot water stored to keep it at a constant temperature of about 60 °C. › Fig. 22 The water is heated directly by a connected heat source or indirectly by a heat carrier, which could be an antifreeze solution in a thermal solar installation. › Chapter Hot water systems, Solar heating of hot water

Hot water storage must be located centrally in the building near the heating plant. It is thermally insulated and is able to supply several draw-off points as a closed, pressurized system. Open, unpressurized and uninsulated storage systems like boilers are designed for individual draw-off points.

Thermal solar installations can also be connected or retrofitted to hot water storage systems. As the storage and boiler are directly connected in these systems, the boiler reheats the water if the temperature rise achieved from the thermal solar installation is insufficient, or if the temperature of the hot water in storage falls below a particular set level. The disadvantage of hot water storage systems is that the water may go stale if it is stored for long periods.

Compared to instantaneous water heaters, which are located close to the points of use, central storage systems are associated with higher installation costs, as their pipework systems are usually considerably longer and therefore more expensive to install. However, overall costs can be reduced if hot water production is linked with heating the building, as it means only one boiler has to be installed.

Legionella

Oversized pipework systems, drinking water heating systems with large storage capacities or poorly insulated drinking water pipes provide the right conditions for *Legionella* to multiply. *Legionella* are rod-shaped bacteria that are present in cold water in low concentrations but multiply quickly in warm water. Humans become infected not by drinking the water but by inhaling the aerosol created by agitating the water, for example, when showering. The symptoms of the illness are like those of a lung infection, starting with a fever, muscle pain, cough, and severe shortness of breath. It is very easily mistaken for influenza-type illnesses. If the illness is not diagnosed in time and treated with a suitable antibiotic, it can be fatal.

If the water temperature in a hot water storage vessel falls to between 30 to 45 °C for an extended period, there is the risk of *Legionella* contamination. A simple but effective method of preventing the build-

🗋
\\ Note:
Unpressurized, uninsulated storage systems could be boilers or point-of-use water heaters, which are mostly installed as undersurface appliances below basins or sinks. They are suitable for producing small quantities of hot water quickly, e.g. in office kitchenettes.

up of *Legionella* in drinking water is to thermally disinfect the stored water. This can be done by raising the temperature of the hot water to over 60 °C, which kills the bacteria, daily or weekly. Another method is electrolytic disinfection, which works by creating disinfecting agents in the water.

### Solar heating of hot water

Solar collectors provide the most environmentally compatible form of heat energy because it is not accompanied by any emissions. Thermal solar installations are primarily used for the provision of hot water. Depending on the climate and given a favorable building, if the area is doubled the installation can also be used to support the heating system.

Thermal solar installations consist of flat plate or vacuum tube collectors, which differ in their efficiency and manufacturing cost, the fluid circuit for transporting the generated heat using a water-glycol mixture, and the hot water storage vessel in which the water is heated. A heat exchanger in the hot water storage vessel transfers the heat transported from the collector into the water in the vessel. › Fig. 23

The design of the solar installation depends on the selected collector type and whether the intended use is hot water provision alone or also to support space heating.

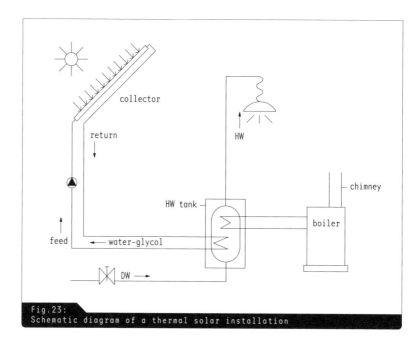

Fig.23:
Schematic diagram of a thermal solar installation

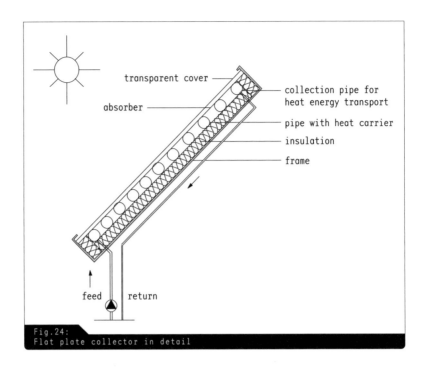

Fig.24:
Flat plate collector in detail

Flat plate collectors

Flat plate collectors consist in principle of an absorber layer with a highly selective coating, which allows the collector to absorb almost all of the solar radiation that falls upon it. The absorber is covered with a transparent cover of non-reflective safety glass with a high solar energy transmittance value and thermal insulation on the back and sides. The whole system is supported on a frame. Pipes filled with a heat transfer medium under the glass cover absorb the heat and transport it to the hot water storage system. › Fig. 24–26

\\Tip:
In a central European climate, a flat plate collector surface area of between 1.2 and 1.5 m$^2$ per person would be enough to provide hot water to residential buildings. Double that area would be needed to provide support to the space heating system in winter as well: 2.4 to 3.0 m$^2$ per person.

Fig.25:
Flat plate collector installed on a roof

Fig.26:
Flat plate collector integrated into a
facade

Fig.27:
Vacuum tube collector

Vacuum tube
collectors

With vacuum tube collectors, the absorber layer is inside airtight
glass tubes to increase efficiency. › Fig. 27 The collectors consist of several
glass tubes arranged close to one another and connected by a special mount
to the collection tube, which is filled with a water-glycol mixture. Vacuum

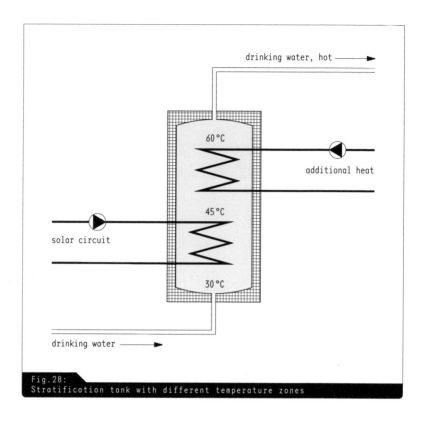

drinking water, hot ⟶

60 °C

additional heat

45 °C

solar circuit

30 °C

drinking water ⟶

Fig.28:
Stratification tank with different temperature zones

tube collectors can be set at a particular angle by rotating them at the time of installation, so that a good yield can be obtained, even if the unit is at a relatively unfavorable vertical angle or less than optimum alignment. Metal plate reflectors attached to the sides can increase the amount of solar radiation the unit receives. The higher efficiency of vacuum tube collector systems means that an area of 0.8 to 1.0 m$^2$ per person is required for hot water provision in residential buildings.

Alignment

Solar collectors are usually integrated into a southeast or southwest-facing pitched roof, or set at a vertical angle of 30 to 45° on a flat roof if they are intended to provide hot water all year round. If they are to provide support for space heating in Central Europe, the angle should be up to 60° as the winter sun is considerably lower in the sky. The units, in particular those with vacuum tube collectors, can also be attached in front of balconies, facades or similar alternative positions. If, for constructional reasons, the units cannot be installed at a suitable vertical angle or if the roof is not quite facing in the right direction, then a greater collector area should be provided.

If the amount of available solar radiation in winter is small, collectors can cover only part of the annual hot water demand and an additional means of water heating is required. One possibility that could be recommended is a combination of hot water provision and support to space heating. This system stores water in zones of different temperature in a stratification tank and can be used as a heat source for space heating. › Fig. 28

In a stratification tank, the hottest water is at the top over a middle mixed zone, with the coolest water at the bottom where cold drinking water is introduced. The feed to the heating circuit is taken from the top of the stratification tank, where higher temperatures prevail. When there is insufficient solar radiation, a separate boiler provides the additional heat through a heat exchanger. In this way about 25% of the heating energy demand can be fulfilled from renewable sources. Solar installations supporting space heating are most effective using a combination of floor or wall heating because this method of heating requires lower feed temperatures than heating radiators.

› ⋒

## SANITARY ROOMS

Hot water is produced by one of the systems described above, and distributed in parallel with cold water in a system of pipes to be ready for use at various draw-off points in kitchens, sanitary and other rooms with a hot water requirement. Sanitary rooms are mainly used for personal care and hygiene. Of all the rooms in a house, they are the most intensive in their use of building services installations, as they have cold and hot water supply and the associated waste water disposal systems. Depending on their design, they may be termed rooms with wet areas or wet rooms. To cut down the work involved in installing the pipework, the layout of these rooms should be chosen to reduce the number of installation shafts and shorten the water supply and disposal pipes, as far as possible. Grouping the pipes together not only simplifies the plumbing work, but also reduces the transmission of sound to neighboring rooms.

⋒

\\ Note:
Further information on the heating of buildings can be found in the chapter on "Tempering systems" in: Oliver Klein and Jörg Schlenger, *Basics Room Conditioning*, Birkhäuser Verlag, Basel 2008.

Noise from sanitary rooms often originates from WC cisterns, water flowing in waste pipes, faucets drawing off water, or activities in the room. These sounds are transmitted to other rooms through walls, ceilings and floors. Quiet rooms or bedrooms should not be positioned adjacent to bathrooms or toilets if disturbing noises are to be avoided. Walls with services in them next to bedrooms, for example, cannot be insulated to the extent that they emit no sound at all. Siting sanitary rooms next to separating walls between residential properties is only recommended if there is also a kitchen, bathroom or other room where noise is not an issue on the other side of the wall in the adjoining property, unless there is an acoustic isolation joint between the two parts of the building.

Wall chases are not advantageous in terms of sound transmission. Surrounding the pipes in the chases with insulation will certainly attenuate the noise, but the chase then has to be cut deeper, which is usually associated with structural stability problems.

Baths and lavatory pans standing on the floor should be bedded on an elastic isolating layer or a floating screed, so that the noises from them are not transmitted through the floor into neighboring rooms. Wall-hung sanitary appliances such as lavatory pans, wash basins or shelves should be attached to walls with a high mass per unit area using sound-insulating sleeves or plastic profiles or attached to false walls.

Faucets and valves in bathrooms are manufactured in two noise categories: low-noise faucets are category I; those that emit higher levels of noise are category II. For noise insulation, category I faucets are preferable, although they may sometimes give rise to higher costs.

The design of sanitary rooms is always a difficult task for architects, as it involves not only the layout and style but also the sound insulation and the integration of extensive pipework. This calls for great attention to detail, as a poorly thought-out arrangement of sanitary appliances and the resulting awkward pipework routes often cause technical, functional, and financial problems.

### Arrangement of sanitary installations

When planning a sanitary room, an architect must take into account how far the sanitary appliances are from the drinking water risers and waste water stacks, and how directly and simply the connections can be made. While drinking water pipes generally have a small cross section and can even be installed in the floor structure without much problem, waste water pipes are more difficult to incorporate because of their relatively large diameters and required fall of 2% within buildings. Depending on the type of sanitary appliance, waste water pipes often start off slightly higher

Fig.29:
Substructure of a double-sided false
wall

than floor level, which means connection to the stack is easy provided the distance is short.

Exposed drinking and waste water pipes create high levels of noise. On the other hand, false wall installations of various constructional types, or shafts that pass from story to story and conceal pipework, increase sound insulation and dispense with the need for expensive wall chases.

False wall
installations

Instead of attaching sanitary appliances to a solid wall and forming the void around the pipe route with conventional masonry, most pipes are now installed behind false walls to preserve the structural stability of the main walls and provide better sound insulation. They consist of a metal supporting frame and a system for attaching the sanitary appliances. The remaining space inside them is filled with insulation and the frame is clad with plasterboard. › Fig. 29 False walls are normally between 1.00 m and 1.50 m high and are fixed about 20 to 25 cm in front of the real wall, depending on the diameter of the pipes behind them. They conceal only the pipework for that particular story and not pipes from other stories unless they are directly connected to an installation shaft. The top surface of a false wall can be used as a bathroom shelf.

Another version of a false wall installation is the modular assembly block system. This involves prefabricated, compact elements formed from polyester foam concrete, which encapsulate all the supply and disposal pipe connections, inbuilt flushing cisterns and all the fastenings for the sanitary appliances to be connected to them. They are about 15 cm deep and are either impact-sound insulated at their connections to the wall, or stand on supports on the structural floor. The cavities must be walled up or filled with mortar.

### Fitting out sanitary rooms

The size and fitting out of sanitary rooms depends primarily on the number of occupants and their particular needs. The room dimensions of a bathroom, on the other hand, depend mostly on the sanitary appliances to be installed and the required distances between them. › Fig. 30

A separate bathroom and toilet arrangement should be considered for residential units with more than two occupants to allow more convenient everyday use. For a family with more than two children, there should be another shower in addition to the actual bath, as well as a separate WC. In all considerations of the size and position within the building of sanitary rooms, the designer should take into account that rooms with wet areas should generally be close to one another, so that pipes can be installed in groups and long pipes are not necessary to transport the water.

Sanitary appliances need to be spaced a minimum of 25 cm from one another or placed at different heights to allow them to be used without interference. Hence a washbasin, for example, may be positioned with an edge extending laterally over a bath at a lower level. Similarly, there should always be a clear area in front of each sanitary element to ensure freedom of movement. › Fig. 31

Wash basins    Wash hand basins and wash basins differ in their sizes. While small <u>wash hand basins</u> are found in lavatories and are intended for hand washing only, <u>wash basins</u> have larger dimensions. They should allow an arm to be immersed up to at least the elbow. Most are manufactured from sanitary ceramics or acrylic; in a minority of cases from enameled or stainless steel. The top edge of these appliances is normally between 85 and 90 cm above floor level. Double wash basin units are more economic in their use of

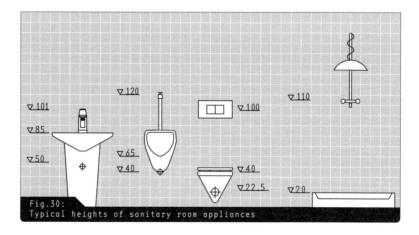

Fig.30:
Typical heights of sanitary room appliances

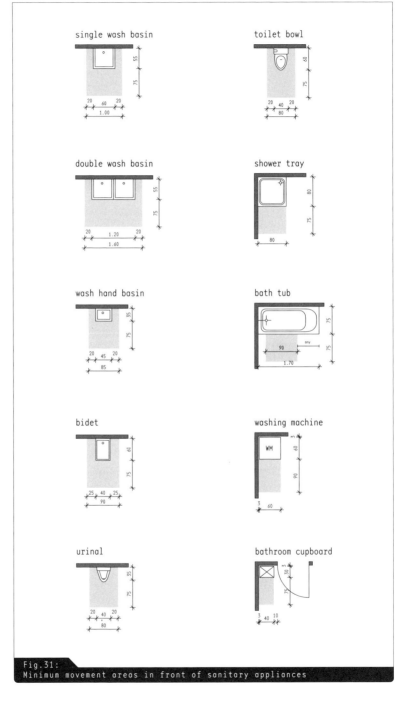

Fig.31:
Minimum movement areas in front of sanitary appliances

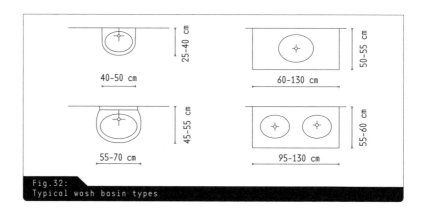

Fig. 32:
Typical wash basin types

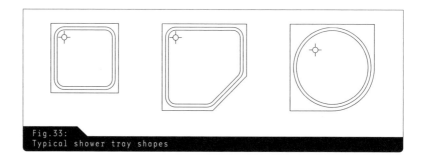

Fig. 33:
Typical shower tray shapes

space than two separate wash basins; however, they must have a minimum width of 120 cm so that two people can use them unhindered at the same time. › Fig. 32

The corner valves for the hot and cold water pipes are installed under the wash basin and are used to turn off the drinking water to the fittings if repairs are needed. It is also possible to conceal waste and drinking water pipes and traps › Chapter Waste water, Waste water pipework in buildings in cupboards or behind panels under wash basins. Wash basins are also often built into specially designed bathroom furniture. This allows better use of the space in a bathroom and provides a more aesthetic way of concealing pipework.

Shower installations

Shower trays are normally manufactured from enameled cast iron, enameled steel plate or acrylic. Various shapes of shower tray are available. They could be anything from rectangular or square to circular or semicircular. › Fig. 33 The standard square shower tray is 80 × 80 cm in plan with a depth of about 15 to 30 cm; larger dimensions and lower entry upstands offer more space and are easier to use. To reduce the step up into the shower, the recess in the floor structure must be made deeper to allow

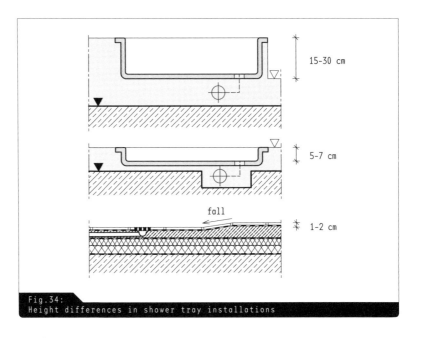

15-30 cm

5-7 cm

fall

1-2 cm

Fig.34:
Height differences in shower tray installations

for the waste water connection, which normally fits conveniently under the shower tray. › Fig. 34 top and middle

Some bathroom designs dispense with the shower tray and have the shower floor at the same height as the bathroom floor. › Fig. 34 bottom This offers not only design and cleaning advantages, but is also part of a barrier-free bathroom. With these wet-room showers, the drainage outlet is at floor level. It is therefore necessary to have efficient waterproofing and edge seals, and a higher floor level to provide the required fall in the waste pipe.

›

\\Note:
The waterproofing and seals may consist of
waterproofing membranes and sealing tape, or
other waterproofing materials, which are spread
on the substrate using the thin bed process.
They should extend at least 15 cm above the top
of the floor covering and brought up even higher
in the indirect spray zone of the shower—even
if the shower is in the bath. They must also
extend at least 20 cm above the shower head on
the walls.

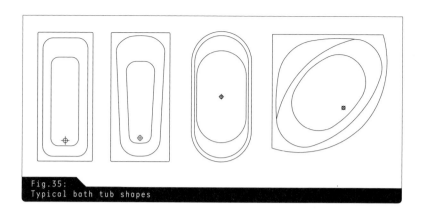

Fig.35:
Typical bath tub shapes

Bath tubs

Bath tubs may be freestanding in the room, placed along one wall and clad in subsequently tiled boards, or set in a preformed foamed plastic bath panel unit. They are manufactured from enameled cast iron, steel plate or acrylic, and are normally 170 to 200 cm long, 75 to 80 cm wide and 50 to 65 cm high. If the entry height needs to be lower, the bath must be recessed into the floor to allow the waste pipe connection to be made. The bath can be made flush with the surrounding floor, for example by building a raised floor plinth around it, as otherwise the floor must be considerably lowered in the area of the bath tub.

The voids between the bath tub and cladding are generally filled with insulation. The gap between the wall and the edge of the bath tub is made watertight with a flexible seal. A clear area of about 90 × 75 cm should be provided in front of the long side of the bath tub to allow unobstructed entry.

Lavatory pans

Lavatory pans can be wall-mounted or stand on the floor. › Fig. 36 The wall-mounted variety simplifies floor cleaning and is usually fixed to special framing members in the false wall construction so that its height can be adjusted. The shape of the lavatory pan depends on the type of flushing process. While older buildings mainly had shallow-flush pans installed, they are now increasingly being replaced by the less noisy deep-flush pans. › Fig. 37

WC flushing cisterns

Flushing cisterns range from false wall installations or exposed pressure chamber cisterns up to wall-mounted, inbuilt or close-coupled cisterns. › Fig. 38 They can be installed at various heights above the pan. While high-level cisterns, which operate with considerable noise, are common in older buildings, new buildings have low-level cisterns or cisterns built into the walls, which are substantially quieter. Pressure cisterns use the pressure in the drinking water pipe and therefore do not require a conventional box-like cistern. The self-closing valve provides flushing water

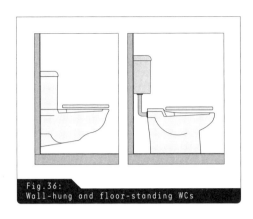

Fig.36:
Wall-hung and floor-standing WCs

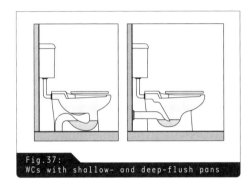

Fig.37:
WCs with shallow- and deep-flush pans

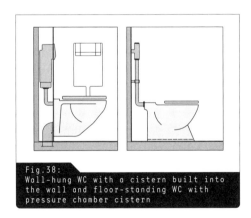

Fig.38:
Wall-hung WC with a cistern built into
the wall and floor-standing WC with
pressure chamber cistern

only as long as it is needed, i.e. as long as the flush lever is pressed. Conventional cisterns, on the other hand, are automatically refilled after every flush.

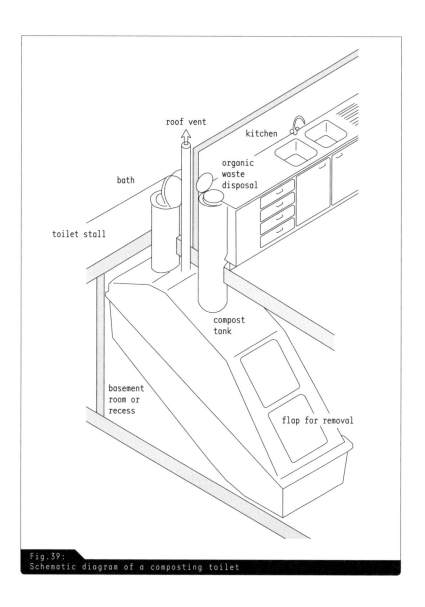

Fig.39:
Schematic diagram of a composting toilet

More than one third of the daily water demand per person, approximately 35 to 45 l, is used for toilet flushing. Reducing consumption of water for flushing offers great potential for saving drinking water. Older cisterns use between 9 and 14 l water per flush, while modern toilet systems require about 6 l. The quantity of flushing water can be set by adjusting the filling height in the cistern. It should also be possible to interrupt the flushing process by pressing the flushing button a second time (water-saving button). To reduce the quantity of water used per flush to as low as 3 l requires the cistern to be connected to a special type of lavatory pan, as otherwise noise may become a nuisance.

Vacuum toilets Vacuum toilets need only 1.2 l water per flush. They have a history of use on board modern high-speed trains and ships. In residential buildings a pump sucks out the contents of the toilet and delivers it into a ventilated waste water tank. From there it is transported by another pump to the public drainage system. The lower drinking water consumption achieved using the vacuum process could result in high savings of waste water disposal charges. The smaller pipe cross sections make installation of vacuum toilets problem-free. However, the flushing process itself is considerably noisier than other types of WC systems.

Composting toilets Composting toilets do not use any water for flushing and therefore produce no waste water. They are used for ecological reasons or because the building is not connected to the public sewer. These toilets consist of a tank with one connected shaft for organic kitchen waste and one for toilet waste. › Fig. 39 Constant underpressure in the composting tank means that no odors can escape into the rooms. The decomposition of the material in the tanks over a period of months is initiated by air flowing through it. The nutrients resulting from this composting process can be used for soil improvement and plant food in the garden.

### Fittings

The term fittings covers all shut-off devices fitted to a drinking water supply system such as stopcocks, gate valves or stop valves, as well as sanitary fittings on wash basins and showers, for example. Shut-off valves block or allow flow along lengths of pipework; they differ in the way they close off the pipe. Stop valves divide up a drinking water system into logical sections to allow parts of the system to be isolated and individual components replaced. Stop valves are therefore fitted before and after the water meter, filter and pressure reducer › Fig. 40 or at the lowest point of each riser and pipe supplying each story. In this way components can be replaced without having to shut down the whole pipe network. Stop valves are also installed at WC cisterns and under wash basins.

Wall- and surface-mounted faucets Tap fittings in sanitary rooms are available as wall- or surface-mounted. › Fig. 41 Wall-mounted faucets, which are mainly installed at bath tubs or showers, are fitted directly on to the wall concealing the water supply pipes, where a short connection piece is used to connect to the drinking water pipework. Surface-mounted models are attached directly to the top of the wash basin or sink and connected to the drinking water supply by means of corner stop valves. The type of tap fitting depends on the intended use; kitchen faucets, for example, have a longer spout then bathroom faucets.

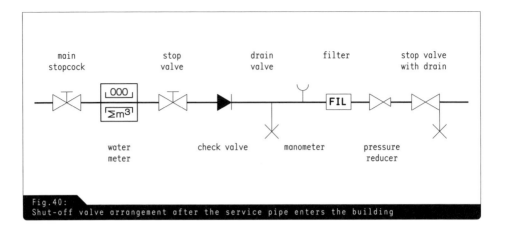

Mixers

Conventional mixers consist of two rotating handles positioned close to one another; with the right and left handles controlling the cold and hot water flow respectively. The user controls the water temperature manually by adjusting the flow of each. More practical are the single lever mixers, which control the water temperature by rotation and the flow by an up or down movement of the lever.

Contactless wash basin faucets

Contactless wash basin faucets are often installed in public toilets for reasons of hygiene. The movement of a hand in front of an infrared sensor opens the valve. Some electronically controlled versions just require a hand to go near the faucet to activate the water flow. A water flow regulator ensures that a constant amount of water issues from the tap. Contactless wash basin faucets require a source of electricity to work. This may be provided by batteries or an external power supply.

Thermostatic faucets

Thermostatic faucets allow the temperature of the water to be preset by a rotating handle, so that the water temperature remains constant even if the rate of flow alters. The faucet mixes hot and cold water at the correct ratio to achieve the set temperature. › Fig. 42

> ⋒

⋒
\\ Note:
All faucets and sanitary appliances should be aligned with the tile grid in the room to produce a pleasing appearance. Faucets should be positioned at a tile joint, a joint intersection, or in the center of a tile.

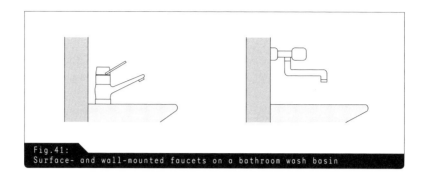

Fig.41:
Surface- and wall-mounted faucets on a bathroom wash basin

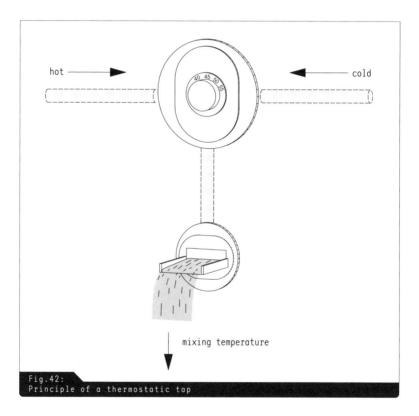

hot &rarr; &larr; cold

40 45 50 55

mixing temperature

Fig.42:
Principle of a thermostatic tap

**Barrier-free sanitary rooms**

Barrier-free sanitary rooms have to satisfy special conditions. They should be fitted out in such a way that the occupant can use facilities in the room without help from another person. To achieve this there should be an adequate and barrier-free movement area of 120×120 cm in front

of the wash basin, WC, shower and bath tub; for wheelchair use it would need to be at least 150×150 cm. Stepless shower trays level with the floor, wash basins that wheelchair users can drive under, and grab handles near all sanitary appliances make their use much easier. The door should have a clear opening width of at least 80 to 90 cm and should open outwards so as not to interfere with access to the sanitary appliances in the room.
> Fig. 43

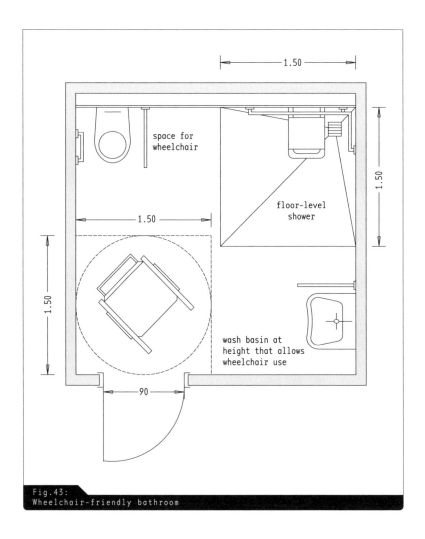

Fig.43:
Wheelchair-friendly bathroom

# WASTE WATER

After it has been distributed through the building's network of pipes, drinking water is automatically changed into waste water when it flows out of the faucets at draw-off points into wash basins, showers or bath tubs, even though it might be absolutely unused and clean. The description "drinking water" ceases to apply as soon as the water enters the waste water pipework.

The term "waste water" generally covers not only water that has become contaminated by domestic, commercial or industrial use but also relatively clean precipitation water (rain). Waste water is usually contaminated by solid particles, bacteria or chemicals, and must therefore be thoroughly treated before it can be fed back into natural bodies of water. This process is normally carried out at the public waste water treatment works.

Heavily contaminated domestic waste water from toilets and dishwashers that contains fecal and putrefactive substances is known as <u>black water</u>. Less heavily contaminated waste water from wash basins, showers and bath tubs is called <u>gray water</u> and contains only about one third the contaminants as black water. This difference is immaterial for the normal process of waste water treatment at the sewage works is concerned, as the plants are generally designed to purify black water. This difference is, however, very important for natural waste water treatment processes, as some facilities can only treat gray water.

Increasing awareness of our environment has shifted the focus, for several years now, to protecting the purity of groundwater, rivers and lakes. The biological self-cleaning process does not work above a certain level of contamination, so that waste water treatment methods of purifying heavily polluted industrial and domestic water are of the utmost importance in counteracting ecological damage. › Chapter Waste water, Methods of waste water treatment

\\ Example:
A four-person household in Germany introduces about 100 kg of detergent into the sewage system. The development of more environmentally friendly detergents has lowered the pollutant load, but has only slightly reduced the problem.

But before treatment can take place, the used cold and hot water must be transported from sanitary rooms in buildings and fed into the public drainage system. This takes place through the pipe network described in the section below.

## WASTE WATER PIPEWORK IN BUILDINGS

Waste water pipes are considerably larger than drinking water pipes and have the task of taking rain and dirty water away from buildings and conducting it into the sewers. A branched network of pipes of different sizes is required ensure that the sanitary appliances continue to work without problems. Buildings are generally designed to be drained by gravity, so all pipes are either vertical or are installed at a fall of at least 2% to transport the waste water down and out of the building. It is important that the waste water does not back up in the system.

> 🛈
Flood level

The flood level is the maximum possible level up to which waste water may rise at a particular location in a drainage system. › Fig. 44 Normally the top of the road surface or the top of the curb at the connection point can be taken to be the flood level, unless indicated otherwise by the local flood prevention authority. This is the limit to which the water will rise in the event of a flood, and therefore it cannot back up any higher inside the building. A flood is most likely to occur during periods of heavy rain. Combined drainage systems are particularly at risk because they carry waste water and rainwater together. › Chapter Waste water, Methods of waste water treatment Flooding also occurs in separate drainage systems, for example if pipes become blocked.

In connected sanitary appliances that are below the official flood level in basements, there is always a risk that waste water from the drainage system will enter the building and cause serious damage. For this reason, each connection point must be protected with an anti-flooding valve

🛈

\\ Note:
If waste water backs up it is possible for the waste water in the public sewer to enter the building's pipework system connected to it, based on the principle of communicating vessels: if vessels or pipes that contain liquid and are open at the top are connected to one another, the level of the liquid will be at the same height in both—irrespective of their shape.

🛈

\\ Note:
European Standard EN 12056 applies to gravity drainage systems inside buildings. EN 752 applies to systems outside buildings. Both standards set out a general framework, which requires national annexes and allows regional departures.

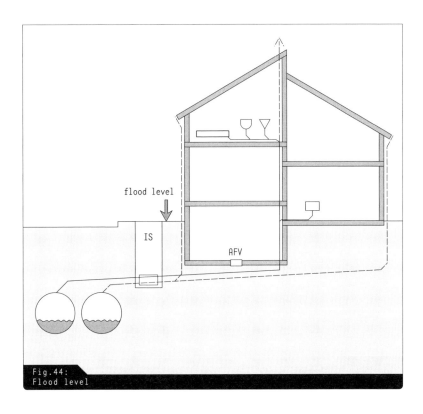

flood level

IS

AFV

Fig.44:
Flood level

or a waste water lifting plant. › Chapter Waste water pipework in buildings, Protective measures, p. 60

### System components and pipe runs

Individual and common waste pipes

A pipework system is made up of many different components, which are connected together to conduct waste water into the public drainage system. › Fig. 45 An <u>individual waste</u> pipe connects each sanitary appliance to a <u>common waste</u>, into which all the wastes in a sanitary room are brought together. › Fig. 46 The common waste has a fall of 2% and takes the shortest route to the vertical <u>stack</u>, which in turn carries the waste water downwards in a uniform diameter pipe with as straight an alignment as possible. The fall in horizontal waste water pipes is necessary to ensure that the flowing water leaves behind no residues in the pipe. All pipes are normally connected into the discharge pipe by 45° bends in the direction of flow to prevent water building up at the connection point. Neighboring common waste pipes must have staggered connections into the vertical stack to prevent water in one from entering the other. The individual

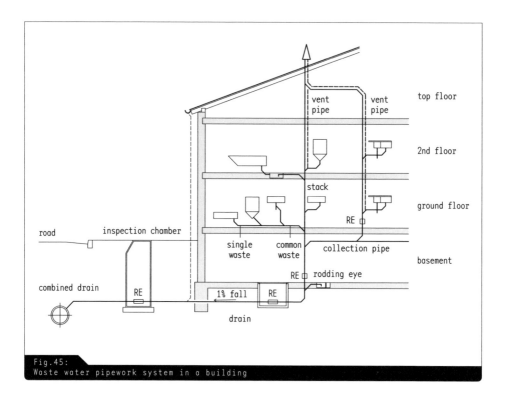

Fig.45:
Waste water pipework system in a building

Image labels: vent pipe, vent pipe, top floor, 2nd floor, stack, ground floor, RE, road, inspection chamber, single waste, common waste, collection pipe, basement, RE, rodding eye, combined drain, RE, 1% fall, RE, drain

pipework system components may be screwed together, solvent welded, or have push-fit connections.

The vertical stack pipe normally discharges below the level of the building's floor slab into a <u>drainage pipe</u>, which leads to the public drainage system or sewer. The stack must be vented to prevent backflow into sanitary appliances. This backflow is caused by underpressure in the stack resulting from the pressure differences that occur when the stack is suddenly used by several appliances at once. If the total length of stack is more than 4 m, it obviously runs through more than one story, and must therefore vent into the open air above the sanitary appliances in the top story and roof level without any reduction in cross section. Alternatively it could be fitted with a venting valve below roof level specially designed for waste water pipes. If the venting pipe is led through the roof to the open air, it must be at least 2 m away from a dormer window or roof window, or must project 1 m above the highest point of these features, so that no unpleasant odors can enter the building from the waste pipe.

At the lowest point of the stack, a drain sufficiently deep underground so as to be frost-free transports the waste water from the building into the

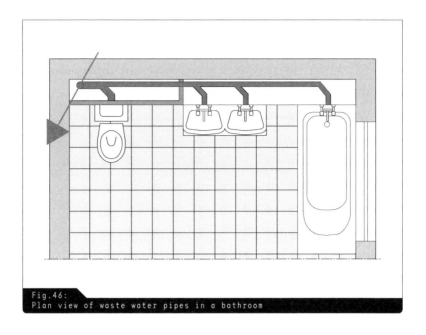

Fig.46:
Plan view of waste water pipes in a bathroom

connection drain, which is connected directly into the public sewer. If an ordinary buried drain is out of the question because the building has a basement and the public drainage system is too high to allow a normal connection, a collection drain can be laid to a fall below the basement floor slab.

Access for cleaning

Only junctions with angles of up to 45° are permitted in buried and collection drains so that waste water can flow smoothly away. In addition, rodding eyes or similar openings must be provided at least every 20 m to allow any length of pipe to be unblocked and cleaned out without excessive effort. In vertical stacks, there must be a suitable cleaning opening at the lowest point, because this is where a blockage is likely to occur first.

Informative signage

The position under the road of drains in the public waste water drainage system is indicated by sign plates usually fixed to building walls or marker posts. The numbers give the direction and distance of connection drains.

Drawing symbols

Various symbols are used in plan and sectional views of planned waste water systems to improve the readability of the drawings and to show the numbers and arrangement of the connected sanitary appliances. › Fig. 47 In a similar way to that described in the chapter on water supply, the drawings should show the true position of objects in plan marked with the appropriate symbol in conjunction with the pipework system. The pipework system, including the pipe layout and sanitary appliances, is shown in a schematic sectional view as if the wash basins, showers, bath tubs or

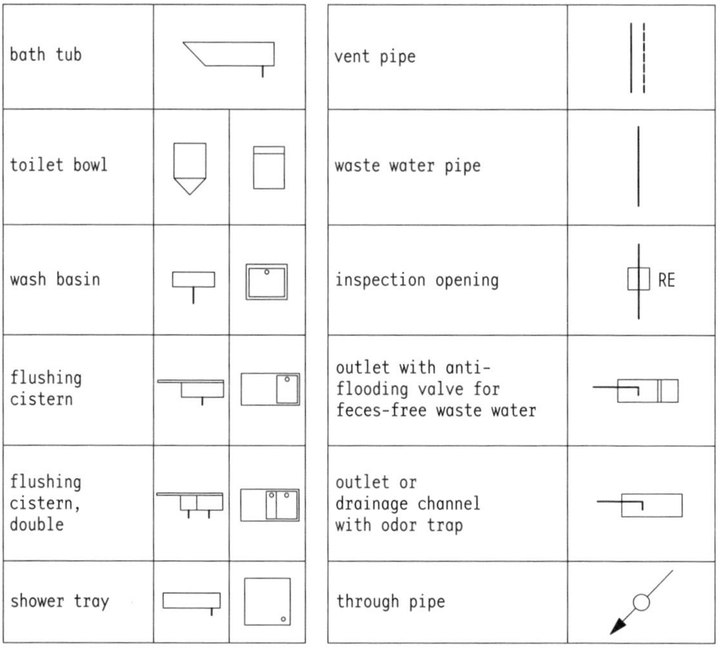

| | | | | | |
|---|---|---|---|---|---|
| bath tub | ◺ | | vent pipe | ‖ |
| toilet bowl | ⬡ | ⬜ | waste water pipe | │ |
| wash basin | ⬜ | ⬜ | inspection opening | ⬜ RE |
| flushing cistern | ⬜ | ⬜ | outlet with anti-flooding valve for feces-free waste water | ⊏⊐ |
| flushing cistern, double | ⬜ | ⬜ | outlet or drainage channel with odor trap | ⊏⊐ |
| shower tray | ⬜ | ⬜ | through pipe | ⟋ |

Fig. 47:
Representation and explanation of commonly used symbols

WCs were adjacent to one another and all connected to a single common waste. › Fig. 45 The pipes are shown with the 45° bends mentioned above, appropriately arranged for the actual direction of flow.

### Calculation of pipe sizes

The cross section of the pipes depends on the type and number of connected sanitary appliances and the water demand, which in turn depends on the desired level of comfort and convenience in the building. Each appliance that generates waste water has a connection value (DU) and a minimum required pipe cross section. › Tab. 6 The estimated waste water outflow ($Q_{ww}$) in liters per second (l/s) of an appliance is the most important parameter in calculating the required nominal pipe size in waste water systems. The drainage index (K) is a measure of the frequency with which a waste water appliance is used. Hence the design of the system will vary with the type and use of the building. For example, sanitary installations in schools or public buildings will be much more frequently used than those in residential buildings.

| Waste water appliance | Connection value (DU) | Pipe diameter |
|---|---|---|
| Wash basin | 0.5 | DN 40 |
| Shower with plugged outlet | 0.8 | DN 50 |
| Shower with unplugged outlet | 0.6 | DN 50 |
| Bath tub | 0.8 | DN 50 |
| WC with 6-liter cistern | 2.0 | DN 100 |
| WC with 4- to 5-liter cistern | 1.8 | DN 80 to DN 100 |

The sum of the connection values of each appliance is used to calculate the pipe cross section of the common waste, stack or drain pipe. Therefore the required size of the drain is calculated from the sum of the connection values of all the waste water generating appliances connecting into it. A horizontal waste water pipe to which a WC is connected, for example, usually requires a nominal pipe size of at least DN 100; which means a pipe with an internal diameter of 100 mm. The vertical stack must therefore also have a diameter of at least DN 100. For a series of connections into a pipe, the total connection value can be calculated using the following formula:

$$Q_{ww} = K \times \sqrt{\Sigma \ (DU)} \text{ in l/s.}$$

$Q_{ww}$ = Quantity of waste water (waste water outflow);
DU  = Design units (connection value);
K   = dimensionless drainage index, which represents the frequency of use (in residential buildings 0.5; in schools, restaurants, hotels 0.7; in public buildings with frequent usage 1.0).

### Materials

Waste water pipes can be made from vitrified clay, cast iron, steel, fiber cement or plastic, while rainwater downpipes may be manufactured from lead. Vitrified clay pipes are generally used for buried drains, as they are resistant to load. Cast iron and fiber cement pipes are suitable for all types of building and land drainage systems. Their high mass per unit

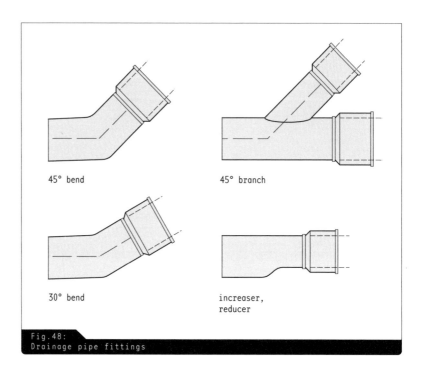

45° bend

45° branch

30° bend

increaser,
reducer

Fig.48:
Drainage pipe fittings

area makes them particularly useful for attenuating the noise of flowing waste water. Steel or stainless steel pipes are used where the waste water they carry is corrosive, which might be the case in laboratories, for example. The most economic material is plastic. Low weight and corrosion resistance means plastic pipes are primarily used in residential buildings, with higher-quality plastic pipes also finding use in industrial and commercial buildings. The plastic used for all pipe components must be heat-resistant.

All materials are produced in short standard lengths and connected to one another by push-fit sleeves, threaded or sealed connections or, in the case of rainwater downpipes, crimped or soldered. They can be obtained as bends, branches, increasers and in other shapes. › Fig. 48

### Protective measures

Odor traps

Traps ensure that no unpleasant odors can escape from waste water pipes into rooms. They are fitted below the outlet of each sanitary appliance. Traps are available in various forms, but they all work on a similar principle to the pipe odor trap, which is the most popular due to its excellent flow characteristics. It consists of a curved piece of pipe of at least 30–45 mm diameter, which retains some water in its bend. › Fig. 49, left The

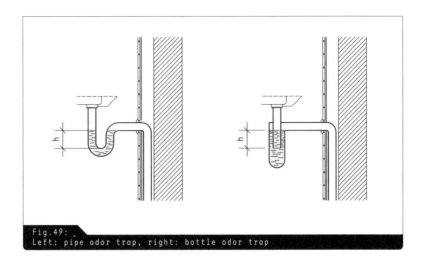

Fig.49:
Left: pipe odor trap, right: bottle odor trap

bottle trap is more prone to blocking and therefore is less popular. › Fig. 49, right The standing water in double traps prevents odors from escaping out of the pipe into the room.

Floor outlets It is prudent to build floor waste water outlets in bathrooms in residential properties where washing machines or floor level showers are installed. They are specified for use in public buildings or swimming pools. They may be manufactured from cast iron, stainless steel, brass or plastic; they can be installed in the floor structure and require the least possible installation depth. When these floor outlets are installed, the floor must have a slight fall of 1.5% towards the outlet and be sealed so as to be waterproof. › Fig. 50 As the floor outlet is often in the middle of the room, it is not always an easy task to lead the connected waste pipe to the nearest stack. These outlets are usually only connected to DN 50 or perhaps DN 70 waste pipes, but they must be laid with the normal 2% fall.

Anti-flooding valves As discussed earlier with reference to flood level, all waste water appliances that are below the flood level must have tightly sealing anti-flooding valves to prevent the backflow of foul water into the building. This may happen, in particular with combined drainage systems, when heavy rain takes the flow in the public drainage system to its limit. A high water level in the public drains can cause waste water from deep connection pipes to emerge from sanitary appliances. › Fig. 51

Anti-flooding valves usually consist of a motor-driven shut-off valve, a pneumatic gate valve, or an automatic or manually actuated stop valve (emergency shut-off). However, all the waste water pipes in the stories above flood level must not discharge through the anti-flooding valve, but

61

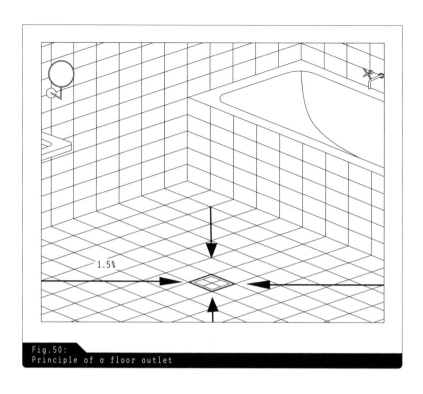

Fig.50:
Principle of a floor outlet

must be connected downstream of it, as the building could otherwise be flooded by its own waste water.

Waste water lifting plants

Waste water appliances situated below the flood level that cannot be connected with an adequate fall to the public drainage system because they are too deep underground have to be drained by a waste water lifting plant. This collects the waste water, which may or may not contain fecal matter, in a tank and delivers it by means of a pump and pressure pipes, through an anti-backflow riser with its highest point above the flood level, into the public drainage system. › Fig. 52 The height of the anti-backflow riser ensures that there is no way for the waste water to flow back into the building. The waste water is then taken in a drain connected to the plant's discharge pipe at the normal fall into the public drainage system.

### METHODS OF WASTE WATER TREATMENT
#### Separate and combined drainage systems

Waste water is discharged into either a combined or a separate drainage system. In a combined system, domestic and industrial waste is led together with rainwater into the drainage system; in a separate

62

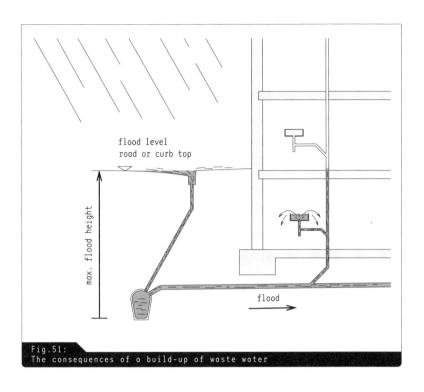

flood level
road or curb top

max. flood height

flood

Fig.51:
The consequences of a build-up of waste water

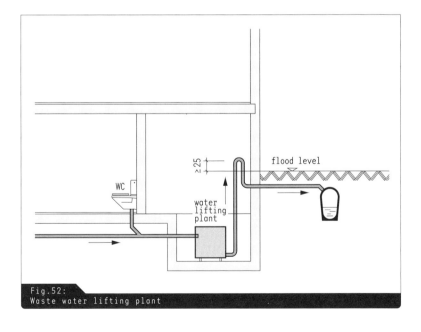

≥25

flood level

WC

water
lifting
plant

Fig.52:
Waste water lifting plant

<u>system</u>, rainwater flows directly into open water or watercourses, often referred to as outfalls, and only the contaminated water enters the public drainage system. › Fig. 53 Within the area of the building and in the design of the drainage pipework, rainwater is now assumed to be dealt with separately from waste water, even if the public drainage system outside below the road surface is a combined system, as many countries are making plans to move to separate systems at some time in the future.

The reason for this is that precipitation water only turns into dirty water when it is mixed with ordinary foul water in combined drainage systems. As a result the volume of waste water increases greatly, which makes changing to a separate system worthwhile to reduce the foul water load on the drainage system and the costs of waste water treatment. The reduction in waste water volumes and the maintenance of natural groundwater levels are two good reasons why rainwater should be drained away if possible within the building curtilage, or be allowed to soak away locally.

Cleaning waste water

Municipal waste water treatment plants first remove the coarse particles from the waste water, and then clean it biologically to kill bacteria and treat it chemically to remove phosphates, heavy metals and nitrates. › Fig. 54 After cleaning, municipal waste water is discharged through outfalls into natural watercourses. But in spite of complex, costly water treatment systems, excessive amounts of plant nutrients and pollutants from treated waste water are entering natural watercourses, where they stimulate increased vegetation growth.

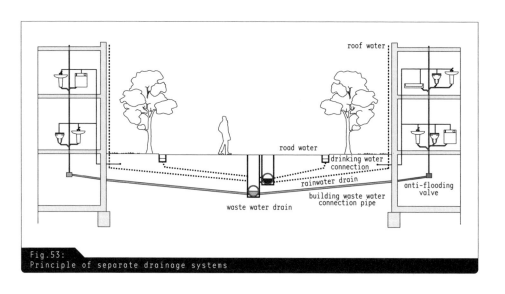

Fig. 53:
Principle of separate drainage systems

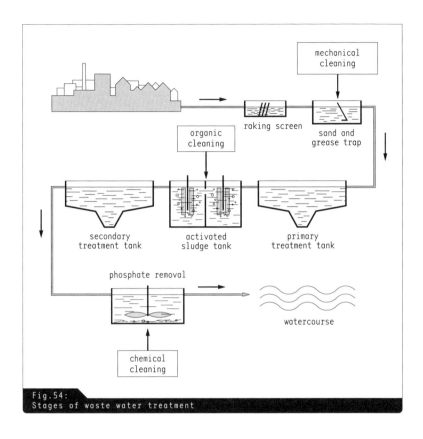

mechanical
cleaning

raking screen

organic
cleaning

sand and
grease trap

secondary
treatment tank

activated
sludge tank

primary
treatment tank

phosphate removal

watercourse

chemical
cleaning

Fig.54:
Stages of waste water treatment

### Natural waste water treatment systems

The idea of cleaning waste water using natural and less cost-intensive methods is not new. Water treatment facilities that work naturally are usually localized, small-scale disposal systems. Similar arrangements have been in use in rural areas for years, where the distance to a public drainage system may be too great to allow a cost-effective connection to be provided.

Increasing problems with the quality and costs of waste water disposal have meant that decentralized, natural water treatment methods have once again been considered as options by environmentally conscious planners over recent years. Numerous ecological housing developments have nearby reed bed water treatment systems, which clean all the waste water generated, within the boundaries of the site. These systems relieve the public drainage system, while sharpening our ecological sense of the natural water cycle and returning the responsibility for it to the individual.

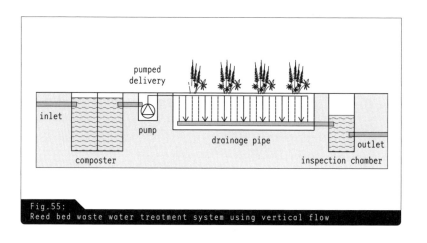

Fig.55:
Reed bed waste water treatment system using vertical flow

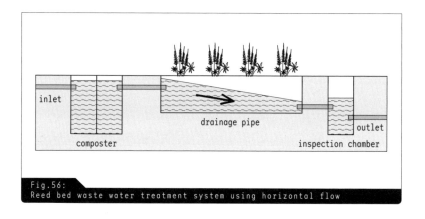

Fig.56:
Reed bed waste water treatment system using horizontal flow

Natural waste water processes have no need for the high energy and installation costs of conventional treatment works, but nevertheless produce excellent cleaning results. The actual waste water treatment process requires hardly any energy input from outside the site, but the systems themselves take up a lot of land. The design of the system largely depends upon the degree of contamination of the water to be treated.

Reed bed waste
water treatment
systems
Reed bed waste water treatment systems are the most common form of natural water treatment. They are generally based around waste water ponds with reeds growing in them and their cleaning effect is primarily produced by plant and animal microorganisms. Therefore it is not the plants themselves that purify the water; it is the microorganisms living in their roots that consume the nutrients in the waste water to produce the

Fig.57:
Retention pond

cleaning effect. The bed of the waste water pond is usually a sand filter through which the water flows either vertically or horizontally. A composting chamber or three-chamber septic tank may be installed upstream of the beds to remove solid matter. A continuous flow of air through the chamber ensures that composting takes place.

First, the slightly soiled gray water from showers and wash basins or black water from toilets is carried along a separate pipework system by gravity, out of the building and through a buried composter, where the coarse particles are removed. From there the waste water is pumped out across the reed bed using the vertical flow principle, which takes up less area but the filter is further underground. › Fig. 55

Horizontal flow, on the other hand, involves a larger area of land but less depth. Here, the foul water flows out slowly across the system and is cleaned through the reed bed. › Fig. 56 The choice of system depends on the available space outside the building. Some waste water treatment methods use both flow types in series to achieve the best cleaning effect.

The reed bed is simply a sand and gravel filter bed. As most of the waste water seeps directly into the soil filter, the area does not look like open water but more like planted ground. The water from multistage systems can be passed through an inspection chamber, in which the water quality can be regularly tested before being taken to an outfall or a retention pond, where it could be used for recreation if the quality is adequate. › Fig. 57 The cleaned water could also be used as service water for flushing toilets. › Chapter Waste water, Uses of waste water

Natural waste water treatment processes require a great deal of space to be able to function properly, especially when used for cleaning black water. However, the aesthetically pleasing appearance and natural

67

value of a reed bed are certainly more appealing than a conventional waste water treatment works. Reed bed waste water treatment systems should not be viewed just as an ecological alternative to conventional treatment processes. A natural treatment system is perfectly capable of handling all the waste water from buildings that are too far from the public drainage system.

### DISPOSING OF RAINWATER

Rainwater is also part of the water cycle in buildings because it flows off roofs and impervious surfaces as dirty water and must be disposed of along with domestic waste water.

The solidly paved surfaces in urban areas prevent rainwater from simply seeping into the ground and becoming groundwater in the natural cycle, as would be ideal. Instead, it is conducted through pipes into the drainage system. › Fig. 58 During heavy rainfall the capacity of the drains is often inadequate, so that more and more foul water mixed with rainwater is flowing untreated into rivers and lakes.

Instead of rainwater being conducted rapidly into the drains, the modern approach is towards slower and more sophisticated systems of rainwater disposal that avoid mixing it with foul water. In choosing a suitable system, the designer must take into account the frequency and quantity of rainfall in the area, the character of the ground surface, and the height of the water table.

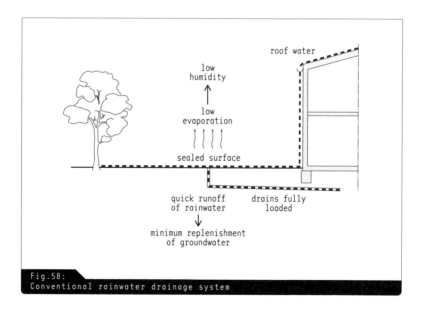

Fig.58:
Conventional rainwater drainage system

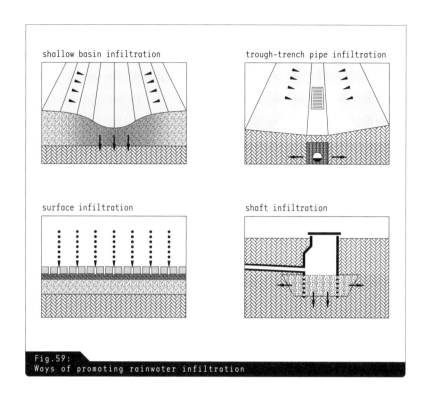

**Fig.59:**
Ways of promoting rainwater infiltration

shallow basin infiltration

trough-trench pipe infiltration

surface infiltration

shaft infiltration

### Rainwater infiltration

To maintain the natural water cycle, ground surfaces that have not been built over, such as open ground, footpaths and squares, particularly in residential areas, should be designed to be as pervious to water as possible, for example as lawns or gravel. This can also be achieved by making built-upon surfaces less impervious so that rainwater can enter the ground in a natural way and contribute to a rise in the water table.

The character of the ground is critical to allowing rainwater infiltration. The more sandy a soil, the more pervious the ground is, and infiltration occurs naturally without any problems. If the soil is so loamy or clayey that rainwater is prevented from infiltrating, special measures may be required such as grass-lined basins, which store the water for a short time, trough-trench or pit infiltration systems, etc. › Fig. 59 These delay the runoff of rainwater and hold back the water in heavy rain, preventing the drains from becoming overloaded and reducing peak water levels. The urban climate benefits greatly from rainwater infiltration.

Costs can be saved in drainage by incorporating infiltration systems on the site. But costs may rise again due to the care and maintenance

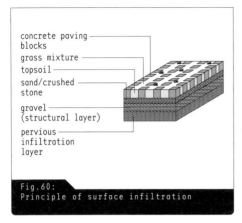

concrete paving blocks
grass mixture
topsoil
sand/crushed stone
gravel (structural layer)
pervious infiltration layer

Fig.60:
Principle of surface infiltration

Fig.61:
Cellular grass paving for surface infiltration

required for more complex retention systems such as green roofs in combination with rainwater ponds or extensive infiltration systems—for example, grass-lined basins.

**Surface infiltration**

With surface infiltration, rainwater seeps into the ground without having to be temporarily stored. Cellular grass paving is one method of surface infiltration; › Figs. 60 and 61 another is water-pervious blockwork; and both are particularly useful for parking spaces, gardens, or little used vehicular accesses. A lawn or gravel footpath can also aid infiltration where the underlying soil properties are favorable. Rainwater undergoes initial cleaning through surface infiltration, even in the top layers of soil. This cleaning effect continues as the rainwater flows slowly through further soil layers until it enters the groundwater.

**Shallow basin infiltration**

Shallow basin or swale infiltration is a form of surface infiltration that delays rainwater runoff. An infiltration basin is a grass-covered hollow in which rainwater is stored for a few hours. › Fig. 62 During this time the water infiltrates slowly into the soil and eventually enters the groundwater.

Shallow basin infiltration requires less land than surface infiltration. With a depth of 30 cm stored water, the area can be estimated as about 10 to 20% of the area of the connected roof surfaces. The rainwater is cleaned as it passes through the various soil layers. Infiltration basins are inexpensive to construct and require little maintenance. Furthermore, they can be integrated as design elements into leisure facilities and green spaces.

**Trough-trench systems**

A trough-trench system combines two methods of infiltration: the grass-covered infiltration basin, and a gravel bed (trench) in which a drainage pipe is laid. The top, approx. 30 cm thick, layer of the basin

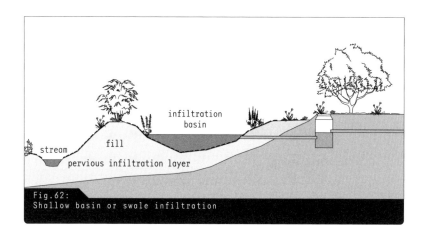

**Fig.62:**
Shallow basin or swale infiltration

acts as both store and filter for the rainwater. On leaving the basin, the rainwater is introduced at a single point or over an area into the trench, which is filled with coarse gravel and lined with a non-woven filter fabric. The rest of the rainwater is transported away slowly through the drainage pipe and is finally discharged at an outfall or into the public drainage system. On the way, the flow is dissipated through the porous pipe so that only a very small proportion of the rainwater arrives at the discharge point. Trough-trench infiltration is also suitable for handling high volumes of water in poorly draining ground conditions.

### Rainwater retention

Retention is the holding back of rainwater. In large towns and cities, many millions of liters of waste water can be saved by holding back rainwater. Retention systems are intended to delay and reduce the direct flow of water into the drainage system. The water is delayed in most cases by green roofs or retention ponds. To an extent, and depending on the construction depth of the substrate, green roofs store precipitation water before releasing it, reduced by two thirds, into the drainage system. They improve the urban climate and in particular the local microclimate. The water evaporating from them can cool hot summer days and bind dust.

Green roofs    Green roofs may be extensive or intensive. While extensive green roofs have a substrate depth of 3 to 15 cm, an intensive green roof requires a substrate some 15 to 45 cm in depth. Both types of green roofs have a separating layer on top of the conventional roof membrane to prevent plant roots from destroying the roof construction. On top of this comes a drainage layer to remove the retained water, and finally the actual vegetation

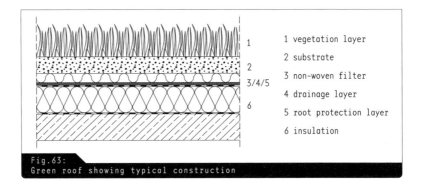

Fig.63:
Green roof showing typical construction

1 vegetation layer

2 substrate

3 non-woven filter

4 drainage layer

5 root protection layer

6 insulation

layer. › Fig. 63 Roofs may be designed as warm, cold, or upside-down roofs, which differ from one another by the position and ventilation of the insulation layer.

Extensive green roofs with a substrate depth of between 3 and 7 cm are planted with mosses and succulents with minimal water and nutrient demand. A somewhat deeper soil construction is necessary for low or medium water demand plants such as grasses or more leafy vegetation. Intensive green roofs consist of faster-growing grasses, perennials or woody species. The greater the substrate depth, the more effectively the roof retains and evaporates water. On the other hand, planting costs and the load placed upon the roof also increase proportionately.

Any flat roof can be a green roof provided that the roof structure is suitable, adequately sealed, and able to support the extra load of the substrate. Roofs inclined at up to 15° require no special safety measures; for more steeply sloping roofs, precautions must be taken to prevent the soil from shearing or sliding off the roof.

Plants and soil layers on green roofs mechanically clean the water. It could therefore be collected in a cistern and used as service water for toilet flushing. Since much of the water is retained and only about one third of the incident rainwater ends up in the cistern, it is normally not economical to install a second pipe network. Above and beyond the general relief of the drainage systems, rainwater retention by green roofs moderates extremes of temperature and improves the thermal insulation of the building during summer and winter.

Retention ponds      Retention ponds generally have beds sealed with pond membranes. Hence they differ from infiltration basins or swales in that they always have water in them. Designed as natural habitats, retention ponds have planted banks and provide living space for a rich variety of wildlife. The rainwater is mainly conducted by small watercourses from the roofs into the pond. The overflow from the pond during heavy rain is often taken to

Fig.64:
Rainwater drainage as a design feature

neighboring infiltration basins. Retention ponds can be a valuable feature in the design of public open spaces in residential developments.

Designing with rainwater

Elements of rainwater infiltration or retention works can also be used as design features to improve the utility value of open spaces and leisure parks. Instead of using underground drains, water is taken along open channels and streams, and can thus undoubtedly enliven the user's overall experience. > Fig. 64

\\ Note:
Suggestions and advice on the use of water in open space planning can be found in: Axel Lohrer, *Basics Designing with Water*, Birkhäuser Verlag, Basel 2008.

## USES OF WASTE WATER

In view of the fact that drinking water treatment is becoming more and more expensive and complex due to the increasing pollution, and yet high quality drinking water is only required in very few areas, it is incomprehensible that millions of cubic meters of rainwater and waste water enter drainage systems without being used. Recent years have seen an increasing number of concepts for substituting rainwater or gray water for drinking water.

### Using rainwater

The use of rainwater saves drinking water and relieves the load on drainage systems and water treatment plants. It poses no risk to hygiene when used for WC flushing, garden watering, and washing machines, as long as it contains no heavy metals or other toxic substances. The quality of rainwater depends on the place where it falls and the character of the surfaces over which it flows. For example, the roof surfaces could be contaminated with street dirt or bird droppings and therefore rich in microbes. The water from highway or car park drains is unsuitable for further use because it may be polluted with gasolene or oil residues. In this case it is better to forgo using rainwater. It should always be possible to

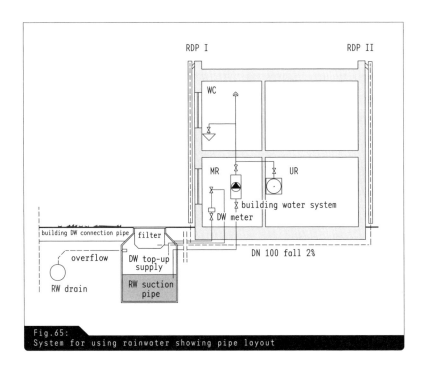

Fig. 65:
System for using rainwater showing pipe layout

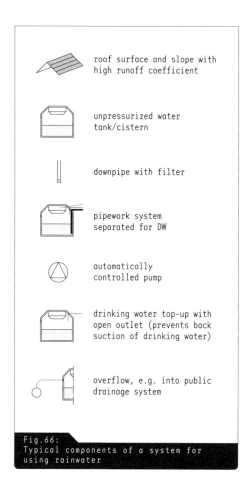

roof surface and slope with
high runoff coefficient

unpressurized water
tank/cistern

downpipe with filter

pipework system
separated for DW

automatically
controlled pump

drinking water top-up with
open outlet (prevents back
suction of drinking water)

overflow, e.g. into public
drainage system

Fig.66:
Typical components of a system for
using rainwater

design the components of any rainwater use system into a building with
relatively little complication. > Figs. 65 and 66

Roof collection area

The size and characteristics of the roof surface used for collecting rainwater are critical to its collection and use. If the roof surface is
smooth, a large quantity of rainwater will be able to drain off, but if it
is constructed from a porous material, part of the water is absorbed and
evaporated. All commonly available roof materials, such as clay tiles, concrete roof paving or slate, are suitable for collecting rainwater. Rainwater
collected from metal roofs can cause graying of washing if a washing
machine is connected to the rainwater usage system. There are no harmful effects if rainwater collected from metal roofs is only used for toilet
flushing.

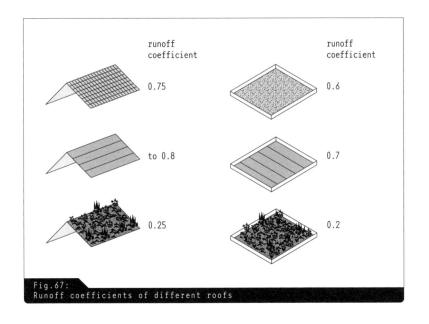

| runoff coefficient | | runoff coefficient | |
| --- | --- | --- | --- |
| | 0.75 | | 0.6 |
| | to 0.8 | | 0.7 |
| | 0.25 | | 0.2 |

Fig.67:
Runoff coefficients of different roofs

The volume of rainwater delivered to the cistern depends on the intensity and frequency of rainfall events and the runoff coefficient of the roof. A runoff coefficient of 0.75 means that 75% of the rain falling on the roof flows through the downpipes and into the cistern. The runoff coefficient is between 0.0 and 1.0 and depends on the roof material. Smoother roofs have higher runoff coefficients. › Fig. 67

Collection tank cisterns

The collection tank is normally a cistern that accepts and stores water flowing off a roof through the downpipes and filters. Cisterns can vary in size and position. Buried cisterns are recommended if the building has no basement. Otherwise the tanks, manufactured from opaque plastic, are set up in a cool, dark basement room, so as to prevent the build up of bacteria and algae in the water. Cisterns are available in various sizes up to about 1000 l. For very high use, either several plastic tanks can be coupled together or a buried watertight concrete tank can be constructed to any size required.

Collection tank cisterns

The design of the storage capacity takes into account the rainwater influx and demand. Regional rainfall maps, which can be obtained from the meteorological office, are used for the calculation of the available rainwater. For example, in Germany the rainfall is between 600 and 800 mm per year depending on the region. The average length of a dry period is about 21 days. The calculation of the rainwater influx is based on the roof area and the runoff coefficient of the roof material.

Calculation of the annual rainwater influx in l/a:

Collection area (m$^2$) × runoff coefficient (w) × annual rainfall (mm/a)

Calculation of the service water demand in l/a:

Daily personal demand × no. of persons × 365 days

Calculation of the required storage capacity in l:

$$\frac{\text{Service water demand} \times 21 \text{ days}}{365 \text{ days}}$$

With a balanced relationship between rainwater yield and service water demand, a storage capacity of about 5% of the annual yield has proved adequate.

During dry periods, drinking water can be topped up from the public supply, through an open, frost-free outlet directly into the cistern, or inside a domestic water station in the building. A domestic water station contains a pump for the delivery of rainwater, controls, pressure regulator, and further safety devices. During topping up, the drinking water pipework must not be allowed to come into direct contact with rainwater, to protect the drinking water in the public supply. It must be possible to conduct away excess water that the cistern cannot accept, through an emergency overflow into the public drainage system.

**Gray water recycling**

In highly impervious inner city areas, where there is generally insufficient space for a reed bed waste water treatment system, a biological gray water treatment system is adequate for cleaning slightly soiled water. They are best installed in a building's basement and are usually an assembly of various system components, specifically chosen and arranged to suit the cleaning process. Which system is installed depends on the amount of space available, the number of users and the budget. With these systems, black water must be separated and led into the public drainage system.

\\Tip:
For rainwater use, the roof area is calculated from a projected view, in this case the view of the roof from above.

Fig.68:
Biological immersion contactor system

Biological
immersion
contactor
systems

A typical biological immersion contactor system consists of a sedi-mentation tank, a mechanical cleaning system in a holding tank, and a bucket wheel, which delivers the gray water continuously in a rotating biological immersion contactor. › Fig. 68 This is responsible for most of the cleaning action, and consists of polyethylene filter tubes, which represent the plant area in a microorganism carpet. The immersion contactor rotates at a speed of 0.5 revolutions per minute and is always half-immersed in the waste water tank, while the other half provides the microorganisms with oxygen by its contact with the air. The continuously growing biomass on the immersion contactor created by this process detaches itself from the rotating body in due course and sinks to the bottom of the tank. After the various purification stages have been completed, the cleansed waste water is no longer putrefactive and can be used as service water.

Membrane
filter systems

Another option for gray water treatment is a membrane filter system, which first mechanically precleans the gray water through a ventilated mesh, using microorganisms and an oxygen feed to remove the organic constituents, and then cleans the water by passing it through several micro-filtration membranes positioned closely one after the other. The membrane filter system is a closed system and can be installed simply and easily into a compact space in a basement room.

Gray water recycling is one of the most environmentally friendly waste water treatment processes. In addition to allowing more use to be made of rainwater, it also ensures that less drinking water has to be expensively cleaned and transported over long distances. Furthermore, the amount of waste water is reduced and the load on treatment works relieved.

If the treated water is allowed to infiltrate, it replenishes groundwater and contributes to the natural water cycle.

The waste water treatment and the environmental alternatives given here connect to the end of the water cycle since the cleansed waste water is returned to natural water bodies. Drinking water recovery and resupply to buildings takes its place at the beginning of the cycle.

# IN CONCLUSION

This examination of the subject of service water shows that there is a wide range of variation in how we handle drinking and waste water, and furthermore that complex and careful planning is called for from architects to integrate a drinking and waste water pipe system, including the connected sanitary appliances, efficiently into their buildings.

However, there is still much more to be done if we are to achieve sustainable development in our use of water resources, as is presently demanded by energy-saving buildings. Comprehensive solutions are required to ensure the long-term stability of the natural water cycle and to avoid burdening it, even if temporary or long-term droughts only occur in rain-starved countries. Instead of developing more and more complex and expensive cleaning and treatment techniques for drinking water, we should be ensuring wherever possible that no pollutants do enter the groundwater. To achieve this will require complex measures that are outside the remit of the building designer.

In this respect, architects can exercise influence on how water is used when they advise clients and point out to them the range of possibilities within their buildings—not only concerning a beautifully designed bathroom, but also how water could used more sparingly and reduce the volume of waste water produced. Simple measures to reduce drinking water usage, such as water-saving faucets or more extensive arrangements for the use of rainwater, different ways of using waste water, and rainwater recycling offer environmentally friendly alternatives to conventional fresh water and waste water technology. Moreover, they promote the sustainable protection of our valuable drinking water resources. In the future, if on the grounds of costs and environmental protection alone, further developments in this area will place great emphasis on water and energy savings. Systems that use solar energy to heat drinking water support this principle. If the will is there, concepts for rainwater and gray water use can be implemented quickly and easily. Overall, these measures make a major contribution to the protection of watercourses and the stabilization of the water cycle, even if, individually, they may appear to have no great effect.

# APPENDIX

## LITERATURE

John Arundel: *Sewage and Industrial Effluent Treatment*, Blackwell Science, Oxford/Malden, MA, 2000

Tanja Brotrück: *Basics Roof Construction*, Birkhäuser Verlag, Basel 2007

Committee on Public Water Supply Distribution Systems, National Research Council of the National Academies: *Drinking Water Distribution Systems: Assessing and Reducing Risks*, National Academies Press, Washington, DC, 2006

Klaus Daniels: *Technology of Ecological Building*, Birkhäuser Verlag, Basel 1997

Herbert Dreiseitl, Dieter Grau (eds.): *New Waterscapes—Planning, Building and Designing with Water*, Birkhäuser Verlag, Basel 2005

Herbert Dreiseitl, Dieter Grau, Karl Ludwig (eds.): *Waterscapes—Planning, Building and Designing with Water*, Birkhäuser Verlag, Basel 2001

Gary Grant: *Green Roofs and Facades*, IHS BRE Press, Bracknell 2006

Institute of Plumbing (ed.): *Plumbing Engineering Services. Design Guide*, Institute of Plumbing, Hornchurch 2002

Margrit Kennedy, Declan Kennedy (eds.): *Designing Ecological Settlements: Ecological Planning and Building*, Cap. Water, Reimer Verlag, Berlin 1997

Heather Kinkade-Levario: *Design for Water: Rainwater Harvesting, Stormwater Catchment and Alternate Water Reuse*, New Society Publishers, Gabriola Island, BC, 2007

Axel Lohrer: *Basics Designing with Water*, Birkhäuser Verlag, Basel 2008

Frank R. Spellman: *Handbook of Water and Wastewater Treatment Plant Operations*, Lewis Publishers, Boca Raton, FL, 2003

Ruth F. Weiner, Robin A. Matthews: *Environmental Engineering*, 4th ed., Butterworth-Heinemann, Amsterdam/London 2003

Bridget Woods-Ballard et al.: *The SUDS Manual*, CIRIA, London 2007

## TECHNICAL STANDARDS

| EN 752 | Drain and sewer systems outside buildings |
|---|---|
| EN 805 | Water supply - Requirements for systems and components outside buildings |
| EN 806-2 | Specifications for installations inside buildings conveying water for human consumption |
| EN 1717 | Protection against pollution of potable water in water installations and general requirements of devices to prevent pollution by backflow |
| EN 12056 | Gravity drainage systems inside buildings |
| EN 12255 | Wastewater treatment plants, Part 5: Wastewater treatment plants. Lagooning process |

PICTURE CREDITS

**Photographs**

All photographs by Doris Haas-Arndt

**Drawings**

Jenny Pottins

Simon Kassner

Helen Weber

Sebastian Bagsik

Indira Schädlich


THE AUTHOR

Doris Haas-Arndt, Doctor of Engineering, Visiting Professor of Technical Building Services and Building Ecology at the University of Siegen, Germany.

Series editor: Bert Bielefeld
Conception: Bert Bielefeld, Annette Gref
Layout and cover design: Muriel Comby
Translation into English: Raymond D. Peat
English copy editing: Monica Buckland

Library of Congress Control Number: 2008934413

Bibliographic information published by the
German National Library The German National
Library lists this publication in the Deutsche
Nationalbibliografie; detailed bibliographic data
are available on the Internet at http://dnb.d-nb.de.

This work is subject to copyright. All rights are
reserved, whether the whole or part of the material
is concerned, specifically the rights of translation,
reprinting, re-use of illustrations, recitation,
broadcasting, reproduction on microfilms or in
other ways, and storage in data bases. For any kind
of use, permission of the copyright owner must be
obtained.

This book is also available in a German language
edition (ISBN 978-3-7643-8853-9).

© 2009 Birkhäuser Verlag AG
Basel · Boston · Berlin
P.O. Box 133, CH-4010 Basel, Switzerland
Part of Springer Science+Business Media

Printed on acid-free paper produced from
chlorine-free pulp. TCF ∞
Printed in Germany

ISBN 978-3-7643-8854-6
9 8 7 6 5 4 3 2 1          www.birkhauser.ch

# Also available from Birkhäuser:

## Design
Basics Design and Living
Jan Krebs
978-3-7643-7647-5

Basics Design Ideas
Bert Bielefeld, Sebastian El khouli
978-3-7643-8112-7

Basics Design Methods
Kari Jormakka
978-3-7643-8463-0

Basics Materials
M. Hegger, H. Drexler, M. Zeumer
978-3-7643-7685-7

Basics Spatial Design
Ulrich Exner, Dietrich Pressel
978-3-7643-8848-5

## Fundamentals of Presentation
Basics Architectural Photography
Michael Heinrich
978-3-7643-8666-5

Basics CAD
Jan Krebs
978-3-7643-8109-7

Basics Modelbuilding
Alexander Schilling
978-3-7643-7649-9

Basics Technical Drawing
Bert Bielefeld, Isabella Skiba
978-3-7643-7644-4

## Construction
Basics Facade Apertures
Roland Krippner, Florian Musso
978-3-7643-8466-1

Basics Glass Construction
Andreas Achilles, Diane Navratil
978-3-7643-8851-5

Basics Loadbearing Systems
Alfred Meistermann
978-3-7643-8107-3

Basics Masonry Construction
Nils Kummer
978-3-7643-7645-1

Basics Roof Construction
Tanja Brotrück
978-3-7643-7683-3

Basics Timber Construction
Ludwig Steiger
978-3-7643-8102-8

## Building Services / Building Physics
Basics Room Conditioning
Oliver Klein, Jörg Schlenger
978-3-7643-8664-1

## Professional Practice
Basics Construction Scheduling
Bert Bielefeld
978-3-7643-8873-7

Basics Project Planning
Hartmut Klein
978-3-7643-8469-2

Basics Site Management
Lars-Phillip Rusch
978-3-7643-8104-2

Basics Tendering
Tim Brandt, Sebastian Th. Franssen
978-3-7643-8110-3

## Urbanism
Basics Urban Building Blocks
Thorsten Bürklin, Michael Peterek
978-3-7643-8460-9

## Landscape Architecture
Basics Designing with Plants
Regine Ellen Wöhrle, Hans-Jörg Wöhrle
978-3-7643-8659-7

Basics Designing with Water
Axel Lohrer
978-3-7643-8662-7

BIRKHÄUSER

Available at your bookshop or at www.birkhauser.ch

**Now in its second edition:
the trailblazing introduction and
textbook on construction**

BIRKHÄUSER

## Constructing Architecture

Materials, Processes, Structures: a Handbook

*Andrea Deplazes (ed.)*

555 pp., 1740 b/w-ills.
2nd, extended edition
ISBN 978-3-7643-8630-6, Hardcover
ISBN 978-3-7643-8631-3, Softcover

Available at your bookshop or at www.birkhauser.ch